Contents

Page no.

Acknowledgements

Photographs:
Carlos Perreira da Silva for Photos 1b, 4, and 6a.
John Mc Gourty for Photo 3.
Kilian Mc Daid for Photo 24.

Aerial photographs:
Nigel Mc Dowell for Photos 5 and 37.
Department of Defence, Dublin for Photo 7a.
BKS Surveys Ltd., Coleraine for Photo 7b.
Coastal Studies Research Group, University of Ulster for Photo 43.

Kilian Mc Daid and Mark Millar drafted the Foreword map and the figures.

We thank the *Donegal Democrat*, *Coleraine Chronicle* and *Belfast Telegraph* for permission to reproduce the newspaper extracts in Figure 5.

Our gratitude is extended to:

The people of the Donegal LIFE sites of Culdaff, Lisfannon, Portsalon, Downings, Magheraroarty, Narin and Rossnowlagh.

The councillors and staff of Donegal County Council.

Foreword

The Donegal LIFE sites.

Recently I went back to a beach where I had spent many a summer afternoon. I was shocked to see the dereliction which had resulted from a series of storms combined with years of neglect and exploitation. At times like this one begins to appreciate the natural heritage we enjoy. Donegal's coastline has been described as a virtual unending beach and it would be a mistake of major import if this generation allowed these scenic assets to disappear.

The European Union has recognised the value of our coastline with its glorious sand dunes and beaches. Through the LIFE-Environment Programme it has provided funding enabling a series of coastal management projects to take place in Ireland and across Europe. Our LIFE project has enabled a wide range of individuals and organisations to come together and work with Donegal County Council and the University of Ulster towards the common aim of preserving and enhancing the county's beaches.

This Good Practice Guide is based on that experience and provides practical advice for dealing with the challenges facing rural beach

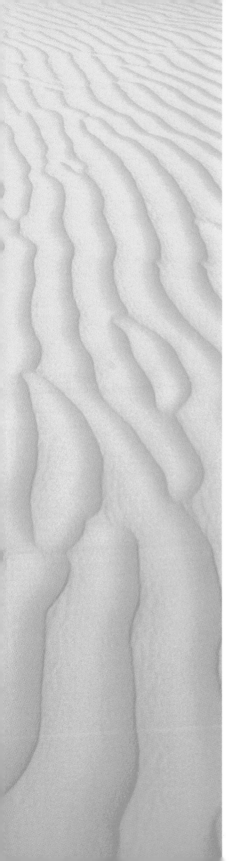

and dune systems. We welcome this contribution from the group and no doubt the findings will be read with interest by all of us who cherish the coastline, whether in Donegal or further afield.

————————————————

Jim Canney
Senior Executive Engineer
Environment Section
Donegal County Council
Lifford, Co. Donegal
Ireland

1. Introduction

Background and Aims

Beaches now, at the beginning of the 21st century, are not used in the same ways as they were at the beginning of the 20th century. Along with other features of our environment, they have undergone major changes in the last hundred years. Some of these changes have had physical origins such as the rise in sea levels, while others have been the result of technological innovations such as the aeroplane, or of socio-economic changes such as the decline of traditional agricultural practices and land uses. In fact, the process of change started long before the beginning of the 20th century. Nordstrom (2000) has described the way in which humans have altered beaches and dunes since antiquity. The rate at which we altered them increased around the start of the 19th century with the onset of the industrial revolution, and has continued to increase since along with "increases in the size and availability of machinery, with development of the internal combustion engine, and with the growth of tourism as a major industry" (Nordstrom 2000, p5).

Alongside these historical changes in the character of beaches have been changes in the way that we approach their management. Over the last three decades or so there has been an increased interest in "green" issues, and a wide-ranging debate regarding our relationship with nature. Part of this debate has involved a reappraisal of the ways in which we manage our environment, and a questioning of previously accepted practice. This has altered the context in which beach management takes place, and terms such as "sustainability" and "biodiversity" are now often used when beaches are being discussed. Beach management often takes place within the context of a regional or national-scale Coastal Zone Management (CZM) strategy (see Brady Shipman Martin, 1997, for Ireland's draft policy). There has also been more consideration given to the role of non-experts in the field of coastal management. Many coastal fora have been established (e.g. the Dorset Coastal Forum in England and the Forth Estuary Forum in Scotland) and the advantages of collaborative and community-based approaches have been highlighted by several authors (see, for example, Kay and Alder 1999, pp136-146). Central to these participatory approaches is the involvement of all those with an interest in a particular coastal area (the term "stakeholders" is often used) in the decision-making process for that area. This book is intended to facilitate the participation of a wide range of people in the management process by providing clear guidance that can be easily understood by a lay audience.

1

The overall aim is to provide a non-specialist text that can act as a first port of call for those interested in learning more about, and participating in, beach management. It is hoped that it will be of use to all those who wish to take part in beach management, whether they are locals, visitors, landowners, academics or those representing organisations such as local authorities or wildlife groups. Space constraints prevent it from being a definitive manual that addresses in detail all the problems that can occur at beaches. Instead it is designed to act as a starting point for practical management by outlining the basic ideas and highlighting further sources of information for those who wish to find out more about a particular issue.

Much of the guidance given in this book is based on the lessons learned in the European Commission, LIFE-funded project "Implementing Alternative Strategies in Irish Beach and Dune Management: Community Involvement in Sustainable Coastal Development", which was carried out in Co. Donegal from 1997-2000 (see Power et al. (2000) for further details). One of the main conclusions of the project was that a thorough appreciation of beach management issues requires some understanding of the physical and social processes that are at work in the beach environment. The detailed discussion of management issues in chapter 4 is therefore preceded by outlines of the geomorphological and ecological processes at work (chapter 2) and a brief examination of the ways in which people interact with beaches (chapter 3). Finally, chapter 5 outlines some of the key steps and considerations for those wishing to devise a beach management plan. The need for management is increasing as rural beaches come under greater pressure from a variety of sources. The problems of rural beaches are quite distinctive and require special management approaches. This book seeks to provide guidance for those engaged in the management of such beaches.

Rural Atlantic Beaches

Although certain parts of the book will be applicable to all beaches, it is aimed primarily at rural beaches, particularly those on the Atlantic coast of Europe. It should also be applicable to areas throughout the world that have comparable physical and social coastal settings, for instance parts of North America or New Zealand. The character of the coastal areas of Western Europe is shown in figure 1. The term "Atlantic" has been taken to include the North Sea and covers the coast from the southern tip of Sweden to Gibraltar. The meaning of the term "rural" can be interpreted in a variety of ways and the definition used here is the one given in the European Commission coastal management strategy (European Commission 1999a). In this an urban area is defined as "a contiguous set of local areas, each of which has a population density superior to 500 inhabitants per square kilometre, and where

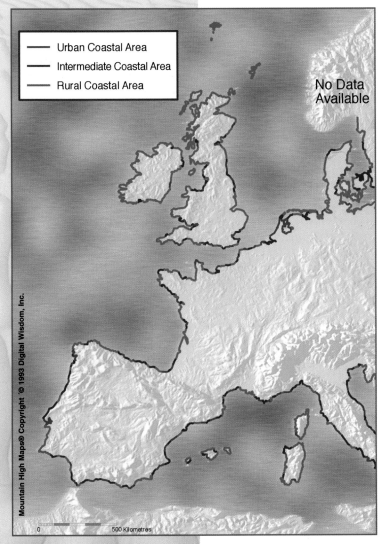

Urban Coastal Area
Intermediate Coastal Area
Rural Coastal Area

No Data Available

0   500 Kilometres

Figure 1. Map showing the character of the coastal areas of western Europe. For definitions of the urban, intermediate and rural categories, see text.

the total population for the set is at least 50,000 inhabitants". An intermediate area is defined as "a contiguous set of local areas, not belonging to an Urban area, but in which: each local area has a population density of at least 100 inhabitants per square kilometre, and either the total population for the set is at least 50,000 inhabitants or the set is adjacent to an urban area". Rural areas are defined as all other areas.

The focus is on rural Atlantic beaches because it is believed that they have certain common characteristics that distinguish them from other types of beaches. These characteristics in turn have implications for the ways in which the beaches should be managed. Atlantic beaches are situated in high energy coastal environments that are characterised by large waves, strong winds and frequent storms. They tend to suffer from high rainfall and consequently erratic patterns of recreational use. They are also subject to larger tidal ranges than would be the case for beaches in the other seas such as the Mediterranean or the Baltic. There is also evidence that the North Atlantic is getting rougher, i.e. average wave heights are increasing and storms are occurring more frequently. Whether or not this is linked to global warming, these changing physical conditions create challenges for beach management.

Rural beaches are, by definition, set in areas of low population density where the patterns of land ownership and usage tend to be different from areas of greater population density. For example, land in rural areas is more likely to be commonly owned or used for agriculture. It is also more likely to be valued for its natural heritage and be part of a protected area such as a National Park or Special Area of Conservation. Although many people, particularly city dwellers, have idealised views of the countryside, rural areas often suffer from social problems such as unemployment, low pay and out-migration. These problems can lead to pressure to develop coastal areas in order to provide employment and encourage

Photo 1a and 1b. These photographs illustrate problems of inappropriate development at Downings, Co. Donegal, Ireland (a) and Monte Clérigo, south-west Portugal (b).

investment. Beach hinterlands often become the focus of tourist/leisure development as they are valued for their scenic and recreational qualities. The effects of this pro-development ethos on beaches can be seen in areas such as south-west Portugal and north-west Ireland where there are many examples of inadequately planned developments such as holiday homes and caravan parks (see photos 1a and 1b).

Because of their greater distance from population centres, rural beaches attract different types of visitors to urban beaches and, in general, fewer of them. The lower numbers of visitors means that rural beaches tend to have less official management, with fewer facilities and less frequent maintenance. This is sometimes offset by the greater willingness of local communities to get involved in the management of rural beaches. It has been suggested (Edwards *et al.* 1997) that rural communities are more likely than urban communities to get involved in coastal zone management initiatives because of their closer association with the natural resource in question. This is important, as local authorities in rural areas do not always have the resources to manage their beaches adequately. In certain circumstances, a beach can appear to be a liability as well as an asset to a local authority. Voluntary assistance can therefore be invaluable, although it should be borne in mind that communities vary a great deal and their willingness to participate, and level of involvement will depend on the nature of the specific community in question.

It could be argued that the nature of the local community is the single most important factor in determining how a rural beach should be managed. A remote beach with few people living nearby is likely to have different management needs from one that is surrounded by a close-knit community where the residents act as informal caretakers or custodians. In turn, both of these will have different needs compared to a beach that has much of its hinterland owned by entrepreneurs and earmarked for development. Rural beach management can therefore benefit from an understanding of

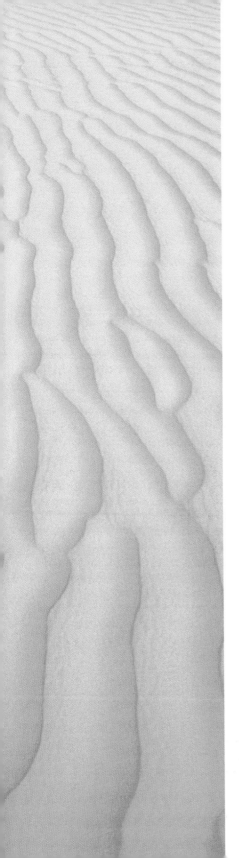

the structure of the local community. Although their involvement does not guarantee success, ignoring the local community makes failure more likely.

It is essential to draw on all the available expertise and enthusiasm if beaches are to negotiate successfully the changes taking place in the rural environment. Patterns of land use, leisure activities, population distribution and physical processes are all in a state of flux and these present serious challenges to those who wish to manage beaches in ways that are sustainable in the long-term. These set the context for coastal zone management and should be considered in the course of developing a beach management plan. The next two chapters examine the role of the human and physical processes at work on rural beaches, and some of the challenges that they raise. This is followed by descriptions of specific management issues and the possible responses. Finally, the guide concludes with a consideration of how to develop and implement a beach management plan. The guide has a practical as well as theoretical focus and draws on actual issues, illustrated with case studies, to show potential solutions and pitfalls.

2. The natural beach–dune system

Effective management of any natural system demands some knowledge of how that system works. This chapter gives a simplified account of the workings of a natural sand beach and dune system. The main elements are illustrated in figure 2 and photo 2. Pethick (1984) gives an accessible account of the physical processes, while Carter (1988) provides a more detailed treatment of both the physical and ecological aspects of coastal systems.

Physical Processes

Photo 2. Foredunes lie seaward of the primary dune ridge at Stocker Strand, Portsalon, Co. Donegal. The presence of foredunes indicates that dune-building processes are active on the site.

A beach is simply the ramp of unconsolidated sediment that is deposited along the shoreline by waves. We often think of a beach as consisting of sand-sized particles only, but strictly speaking a beach can consist of any sediment size capable of being transported by waves. This ranges from large boulders to fine mud. Some beaches consist almost entirely of one size grade but others have a mixture of size populations, e.g. it is common to find a steep narrow gravel storm beach lying landward of a wide inter-tidal sand beach. Dunes form as a result of vegetation trapping and colonising wind blown particles and therefore they are found only where the dominant beach sediment size is sand. As this Good Practice Guide is directed at the management of recreational beaches it will concentrate on sand beach and dune environments.

The morphology (i.e. shape and form) of beaches and dunes results from the interaction of energy (waves, tidal currents, wind) with the available sand-sized sediment. Beaches are created as sand is brought in by waves from offshore sources or from alongshore by wave and tidal currents. Wave action builds the low angle deposit of sand that we call the beach. While no two beaches are alike we can identify certain common processes and in particular a cyclic pattern to erosion and accretion.

Figure 2. The main elements of a natural beach and dune system.

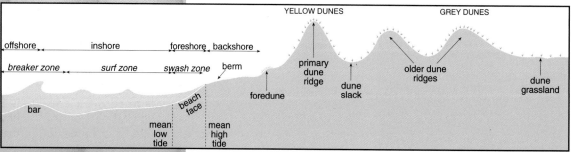

6

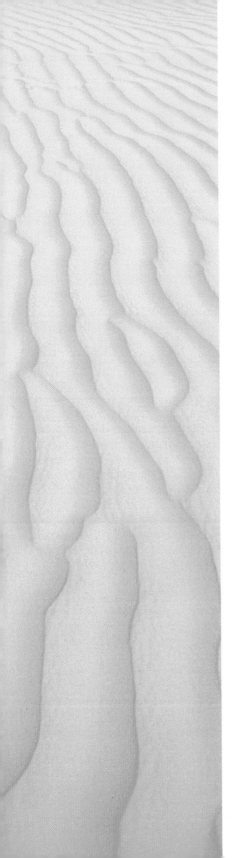

During periods of calm weather long, flat swell waves bring sand onshore. The beach has its maximum sand volume under these conditions and it often has a pronounced crest just above the high water mark known as the "berm". The berm is the source of sand for the dunes that are found landward of the beach above the Mean High Water mark (MHW). A combination of sand blow by onshore winds and the action of sand-binding plants creates embryo dunes and foredunes, leading ultimately to the development of a series of high dune ridges.

Storms have steeper shorter waves that lower and flatten the beach. The berm is removed, the upper beach surface is eroded, and the frontal dunes are cut back as the beach profile now reflects a condition of minimum sand volume. Sand is deposited on the lower part of the profile and in the shallow water just below low tide level. The now wider, flatter beach with a newly formed nearshore sand bar just is ideally suited to dissipate the energy of the storm waves. In the weeks and months after the storm constructive swell waves bring the eroded sand back onshore. The cycle is completed as the upper beach and berm are rebuilt and onshore winds restore the dunes.

It is important to recognise that the shape, size and character of a beach and dune system is the outcome of a continuous, finely balanced interaction of wave and wind energy with sand-sized particles. Any change in any of these factors will result in beach readjustment. As we have seen, a naturally functioning beach flattens its profile to create the maximum dissipation of storm-wave energy. This flexibility and ability to "roll with the punches" is the reason why sand beaches are often described as the best possible means of coastal defence. The system is often a cyclic one with periods of erosion alternating with periods of accretion to give a kind of long-term average position and geometry. While the position and form of the beach show obvious changes pre- and post- storm there is nevertheless an identifiable mean (modal) condition. This concept of short-term fluctuation around a longer-term average position is known as "dynamic equilibrium". Paradoxically it is the capacity of a beach to change that gives it the stability expressed in this term.

Beaches and dunes are fundamentally dynamic, i.e. they must change if they are to function in a natural way. The form of the beach will change as energy levels change. Some of these changes in energy levels are short-term and highly predictable, e.g. tidal variations move wave action up and down the beach slope in a known time frame. The high wave energy levels of randomly occurring storms are less predictable, but nevertheless the beach response is largely predictable. Since change is both inevitable and necessary it is entirely inappropriate to consider erosion as a "problem". Erosion is a necessary and vital part of any healthy functioning beach and dune system. Without the flexibility that

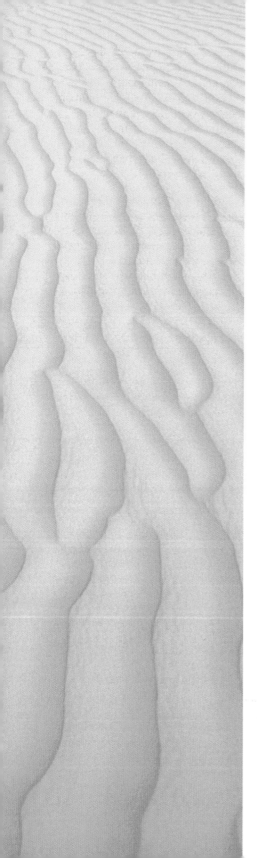

erosion allows the beach profile can not adjust to damp down the effects of storms. It follows that for the beach and dune system to work effectively there must be no interference with any of its components. Destruction of dunes removes the vital backing store of sand required to flatten the beach, groynes prevent longshore readjustments of the beach plan, while seawalls, bulkheads and revetments erect a barrier between beach and dunes thus preventing the two-way interchange of sand that is so important for long-term beach and dune stability. The result of hardening the backshore with shoreline defences can be disastrous, with a serious risk that the entire beach will be lost due to wave reflection and sand scour.

The pattern of cyclic change around a mean described above is not the only type of change. Sometimes short period cyclic changes are superimposed on a long-term trend. There are sections of shoreline where the long-term trend is one of net erosion or accretion. Such non-cyclic changes are termed progressive. On most European coasts today erosion is the dominant theme. The reasons for progressive changes are various: global or local relative sea level changes, increased frequency and intensity of storms, natural or human-induced variations in sediment supply, variations in wave climate whether natural or caused by human interference with the coastal system. In a situation of progressive change the beach system will retreat (or advance) until it reaches a new position where its form will once again reflect an equilibrium between the wave and wind energy inputs and the sand supply.

From the foregoing it is clear that a natural shoreline may be quite stable in the long-term even though its position and form may change in the short-term. However, beaches are threatened by human mindsets that take an inflexible approach to shoreline position. Where stability is demanded, in the sense that the position of Mean High Water cannot be allowed to vary, attempts will often be made to fix and hold the position of the shoreline. Such initiatives are trying to impose unnatural conditions on the beach and dune system. The consequences of interference with the operation of natural processes are unpredictable but usually unfortunate, e.g. rigid coastal defences may collapse catastrophically when some threshold of energy impact or structure resistance is surpassed. A natural shoreline is inherently flexible and consequently sustainable human use must also be flexible in strategy and accept the variation of the landforms created by natural processes. Beach users should also learn to live with progressive retreat where it occurs. A retreating beach will not usually be "lost" if it is allowed to find its new equilibrium position further landward.

Changes also occur to the dunes. Sand is released from the margins of the dunefield by a number of mechanisms: erosion of the seaward ridge by wind and wave action during storms, erosion of the back dunes by river floods and switching ebb channels in estuaries, and sand blow landward. Within the dunefield the wind erodes sand from areas stripped of their protective vegetation cover by a variety of processes - direct wind effects during gales, fires, the effect of animal grazing (both wild and domesticated), and human activities. These areas of wind deflation become linear gullies or larger hollows known as blowouts. Variation is most highly developed in the poorly vegetated and unstable mobile dunes (yellow dunes) near the beach. Landward the dunes become more stable as they become fully vegetated (grey dunes).

The concept of the coastal cell is an important one in effective beach management. Put simply the cell concept suggests that there are stretches of shoreline in which sediment is circulated by waves and currents with relatively little input from, or output to, adjacent sections of coast. An obvious illustration of this is found where sand beaches occupy the heads of deeply etched embayments between projecting bedrock headlands on a compartmentalised coast. There is little linkage to adjacent embayments because the pattern of currents and the relatively deep water off the headlands impedes sand movement. One important management implication of this is that if sand is lost to the cell fresh supplies will not come in from outside to replace the lost sediment. Sand tends to travel further on "unimpeded", relatively straight sections of coast with few headlands, but even here there are well defined cell circulations which reflect the pattern of wave generated currents.

Ecological Processes

The ecology of any beach and dune system is partially a function of its geomorphological setting. In turn, coastal organisms play an important role in modifying and ameliorating physical and chemical stresses, such as sand deposition, drought and surface instability. Sand beaches are rather impoverished habitats, with fauna often restricted to burrowing shellfish, polychaete worms and sand hoppers. The latter provide food for birds that feed along the strandline, e.g. sanderling (*Calidris alba*). Many beaches have associated inter-tidal habitats that harbour many more species, such as rock pools, platforms and outcrops, estuaries and salt marshes. However, this account will focus on the dune habitats found above MHW.

Strandlines or driftlines are accumulations of litter left by the high tide. They contain a mixture of plant and animal material, including viable seeds, rhizome fragments, marine algae, animal remains and human detritus. Driftlines provide sites for sand accumulation because their surface roughness slows onshore winds. As they decompose, they provide excellent sites for germination and plant establishment. For example, they retain moisture and nutrients, and also stabilise surface temperatures much more efficiently than the surrounding beach sand. Driftlines produce their own community of mainly annual plants, such as sea rocket (*Cackile maritima*), orache (*Atriplex* sp.) and sea sandwort (*Honkenya peploides*). If driftlines survive the eroding effects of winter gales and high tides, they become the precursors of vegetated sand dune ridges. Moving landward, the next vegetation zone encountered is the foredunes, characterised by low ridges and sparse, open communities of the sand binding grasses sand couch (*Elymus farctus*) and marram (*Ammophila arenaria*). Sand couch is moderately halophytic, that is it is able to withstand periodic inundation by saltwater. Unlike the driftline plants, these grasses can accommodate burial by sand by rapid leaf and stem extension. The next zone landward is termed yellow dune, where marram begins to form a closed canopy, is tussocky and dominates the vegetation. Marram grass is well adapted for life in sand dunes. Its ability to bind and stabilise blowing sand allows dunes to grow to up to 20-30m in height. Over time, important changes follow the establishment of marram cover, e.g. accumulation of soil organic matter and nutrients, a fall in pH, increased species diversity and biomass. The final zone is known as grey dune, on account of the darker horizon that develops as the soil matures, and also because these areas often develop a surface cover of crustose lichens, e.g. *Cladonia* spp. Species diversity is highest in grey dune. Charismatic species such as orchids are relatively common. Species composition depends on soil chemistry.

Photo 3. Lisfannon on Donegal's Inishowen Peninsula is highly dynamic and an extensive beach, dune and salt marsh complex has developed this century. Sediment starvation has resulted in the recent onset of probably irreversible erosion.

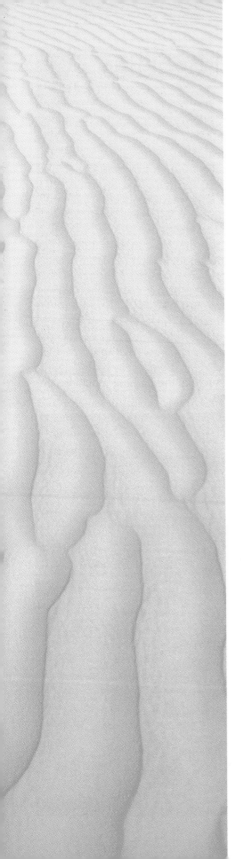

In Ireland, calcareous substrates dominate, producing grey dune communities similar to chalk grassland, e.g. red fescue, wild thyme, purging flax, lady's bedstraw. A particular type, known as machair plain grassland, has developed on the grazed low-lying sand sheets on the exposed northwest coasts of Ireland and Scotland. On acidified dunes, dune heath may dominate. Where grazing has been absent or is of low intensity, dune scrub and woodland are often present, e.g. bramble, blackthorn, sea buckthorn and sycamore. In general, larger fauna are relatively restricted on dunes, although as natural habitats they do tend to harbour a greater biodiversity than surrounding farmland. The most common breeding birds on dunes in Ireland are meadow pipits and skylarks.

In many ways, the transition from open, wave-swept sand beach to fully vegetated dunes is the classic expression of ecological succession (see photo 3). This can be observed on many systems as a pattern from sparsely vegetated embryo dunes to closed vegetation of the landward areas that grades into non-coastal habitats, such as grassland, scrub and woodland. On a few systems, this pattern can be seen as a dynamic process, observable on a scale of years to decades as a dune front prograrades. More common is the reverse process, where progressive erosion on retreating coasts cuts into long-established and fossil dunes that were formerly some distance inland. Some of the classic zones may be present as narrow bands, but these derive from the temporary deposition of reworked material rather than as a result of accretion.

Type of beach interaction	Example of activity	Possible negative impacts
Recreational	Bike scrambling	Noise, danger, dune erosion.
	Beach parties	Litter, noise, nuisance.
	Driving on the beach	Sand compaction, danger, reduction of amenity for others.
Acquisitive*	Sand removal	Dune erosion, beach depletion.
	Vending	Litter, visual intrusion.
	Aquaculture, e.g. oyster farming	Visual intrusion, impact on ecosystem, loss of amenity.
Management	Mechanical beach cleaning	Impact on ecosystems.
	Car park provision in sand dunes	Loss of biodiversity, visual intrusion, loss of dune area.
Educational	School fieldtrips	Litter, dune erosion.
	Nature study	Removal of beach and dune material, e.g fossils or plants.

Table 1 shows the possible impacts of some common beach activities. [*Note that acquisitive is taken to mean any activity carried out for personal advantage, where the beach acts as a source of material gain (e.g. through vending) or lessens the costs that would otherwise be incurred (e.g. by providing an opportunity for free (and illegal) dumping)].

Photo 5. On the top centre right the beach at Carrickfin, Co. Donegal, Ireland parallels the runway of a regional airport.

Photo 6. Two different types of rural beach, (a) Peniche, west Portugal and, (b) Portsalon, Co. Donegal Ireland.

associated with them. In certain instances bye-laws are used to control beach activities and conflicts between users. These may be difficult to enforce in rural settings although they can act as a deterrent. At present, 46 beach-based activities are covered by bye-laws in Ireland (MacLeod *et al.* 2000). Obviously, it is unlikely that all these activities would take place at any one beach. The range of activities and their intensity depends on the characteristics of the beach in question. For example, photo 5 shows the beach system at Carrickfin, Co. Donegal. This site plays a number of different roles. It is agricultural land, a thoroughfare, a scenic landscape, a place for recreation and the location of an airport and factory. These roles lead to a range of demands, which are sometimes in competition.

Case Study 1 (see photo 7)

During the 1960s beachfront landowners moved touring caravans onto an area of dunes which had accreted in the northwest corner of the Trabeg beach at Downings in north Co. Donegal. The beach at that time still possessed a prominent berm and foredunes, and normal aeolian dune building processes were active. From the early 1970s, and accelerating throughout the 1990s, the owners of three caravan sites-which had been developed on the new dunes-constructed embankments of imported fill on top of, and seawards of, the original dunes to fix, defend and ultimately extend the shoreline. Makeshift seawalls and boulder rip-rap were also emplaced to defend the bases of these new embankments. Virtually every spring tide now reaches the toe of the embankments and the beach has been so deflated that it is characteristically flat, low lying and permanently wet even at low water. Dune forming processes are no longer active as there is no store of dry sand available for transport. The stealthy seaward advance of the caravan sites allows the owners to accommodate more caravans, and the extra area acts as a buffer against storms. Only in 1998 did the planning authority issue a warning about this practice. In effect the caravan site owners extended their property seawards of MHW, the legal limit of their ownership, onto State owned foreshore. It is extremely doubtful if the coastal landowners were legally entitled to claim ownership of the new dunes, let alone extend their property onto the foreshore. In Irish law deliberate advance of the MHW line from known boundaries does not bring title. Since the pre-accretion boundaries at Tra Beg were well known the new dunes should have come into State ownership.

(a)

(b)

Photo 7. Shoreline movements at Downings, Co. Donegal, Ireland. The photos show the beach in 1954(a) and 1994 (b).

There are many different types of rural beach, from the busy beach with a developed infrastructure to the undeveloped and unmanaged beach that often has much smaller visitor numbers (see photos 6a and b). These two beaches represent the extremes of rural beach type. At one end is the beach as an amenity, valued for the facilities and recreational opportunities it provides and managed with the aim of providing a clean, safe and convenient place for users. At the other end is the beach as a wilderness area, valued as a natural system and managed in a way that maintains its intrinsic qualities. In between lies a whole spectrum of beach types. Management decisions need to take this into account as the same problem may require different solutions on different types of beach.

The character of a beach is not fixed and it can change in various ways over time. The way in which a beach develops depends on many factors such as: its physical character; its location and distance from population centres; its history of usage; the management regime; prevailing weather conditions; socio-economic context. The main point to bear in mind is that beaches can change, often irreversibly, as the result of human activities (see case study 1). It is therefore essential that the potential longer-term consequences of any activities or processes are examined, as well as the more immediate effects.

Autonomous	The stakeholders control the process and have freedom (within legal limits) to make decisions and set agendas. They are consequently responsible and liable for their actions.
Devolved	Stakeholders obtain some control of decision making and agenda setting within strictly defined limits. The exact balance of power and responsibility between the stakeholders and the devolving authority is negotiated.
Collaborative	Stakeholders are encouraged to become involved in the management process in some way, e.g. by providing input into decision making or data gathering, though they are not given any control of the process.
Consultative	Stakeholders are consulted and their views sought. They are seen primarily as passive participants whose views should, however, be taken into account.
Informative	The stakeholders are kept informed of the management process, but not encouraged to interact with it.
Uninterested	The stakeholders are ignored by those in control of the management process.
Manipulative or exploitative	The stakeholders are viewed either as an obstacle to be overcome or as a resource to be exploited.

Table 2. The different levels of participation between stakeholders and authorities responsible for the management of coastal areas.

Involving people in beach management

Although beach management cannot, and probably should not, seek to change people's values in line with pre-determined norms, encouraging communication between people with different opinions helps to foster understanding of other points of view. This makes it easier to find compromise solutions to what may otherwise be intractable problems, and helps to avoid situations where there is conflict instead of consensus. Conflict should be avoided wherever possible as it erodes the trust and spirit of co-operation that facilitate beach management. For this reason it is important that management activities are explained to beach users (through the use of signs, meetings etc.) so that the reasons for them are explicit and understood. There are many examples of beach management initiatives failing, not because people object to the initiative *per se*, but because they have not been involved or even had the initiative explained to them (e.g. see case study 23). The support of local communities is particularly important in rural areas where a greater sense of ownership of the beach may exist, and people may be more willing to get involved in its management. This may, however, be tempered by a feeling that responsibility lies elsewhere, for example with a local authority. If an initiative is not supported by the local community, then its implementation can become difficult due to the problems of monitoring and enforcement in relatively remote areas.

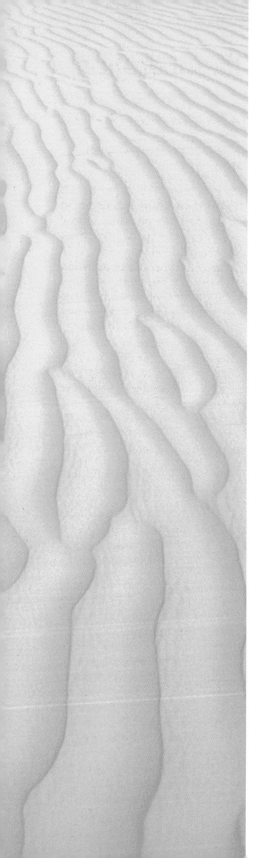

People can become involved in beach management at a number of different levels. At the most basic level this may only mean being informed of what is going to happen. As the level of involvement increases the relationship between the managers and the beach users changes from one where users are informed of decisions, through one where they are consulted, to one where they actively participate in making decisions and ultimately to one where they have an equal say in setting the agenda and making decisions (see table 2). Even if there is no devolution of decision making power, it should be remembered that management benefits from two-way communication in which both sides learn from each other. The appropriate level of involvement depends very much on the patterns of ownership, the type of stakeholders involved and the outlook of the management authority. The desired level of involvement, in turn, determines which techniques should be used to help people participate in the management process. These range from holding open days and carrying out surveys to establishing stakeholder forums with responsibility for managing the beach.

If the decision is made to devolve management responsibility in some way, then a follow-up decision has to be made regarding to whom responsibility will be devolved. This can be a complex decision as there are potentially a large number of stakeholders. Rientjes (2000) divided stakeholders into: *primary* (those whose permission, approval or support is required to achieve the goal; those who will be directly affected by the plan or activity; those who will benefit or suffer losses); *secondary* (those who are indirectly affected); and *tertiary* (those not directly involved who can influence opinions). In an ideal world all stakeholders would have an equal say; however this is unrealistic for a number of reasons. Firstly, the site is more important to some people than to others - there is unlikely to be an equivalence of interest between someone who visits a site once a year and someone that visits it every day or depends on it for their livelihood, such as a landowner. Secondly, people are not always guided by altruistic motives - some may have hidden agendas influenced by other interests. Thirdly, some opinions (including those of "experts") may be based on flawed understanding. There is no easy answer to this problem of deciding who should have what level of say in the management process. Participants have to trust each other's integrity while critically examining their suggestions and motivations. As a guiding principle it is worth bearing in mind that we are merely custodians of beaches and therefore have a duty to manage them in ways that sustain them for future generations to enjoy.

4.1: Issues primarily related to the operation of natural processes

Issue: Beach and dune scarp erosion

Photo 8. Eroding dune scarp on the Dooey Peninsula, Magheraroarty, Co. Donegal.

Description: Storm erosion of the upper beach surface and the frontal dune scarp is a common occurrence on sand beaches (see photo 8). Indeed normal wave action at high water spring tide causes dune erosion at some sites. Erosion may be cyclic in the sense that it is balanced by periods of accretion leading to no net change in shoreline position. However, in many cases retreat of the shoreline is progressive. Buildings and recreational infrastructure such as boardwalk paths, fences, and lifebelts located in the erosion envelope are in immediate danger and may be damaged, undermined or destroyed. Additional public safety, water quality and aesthetic problems result from the damage litter on the beach and from exposed and fractured sewerage pipes and septic tanks. Where streams cross dunes and/or the beach, bank erosion due to a combination of river discharge during floods and wave action at high spring tides may cause lateral shift of the channel.

Response:

Beach managers should recognise that erosion is only a "problem" in human perception. As described in chapter 2 erosion is a necessary process in allowing a beach to survive storm-wave attack. Consequently action to prevent erosion may put the beach at risk.

Attempts to prevent marine erosion are usually made to protect poorly sited development, although there are cases where demands are made to prevent erosion when the only thing at "risk" is natural dune. Therefore the obvious response to beach and dunefront erosion is to avoid locating development or infrastructure on the back beach or frontal dunes. Study of the available documentation, e.g. maps, aerial photographs, academic and consultancy reports, and local anecdote, will help to reveal the mean annual erosion rate, and whether erosion is cyclic or progressive. Frontal dunes can be used but any structures should be temporary and moveable, and made of cheap materials whose loss can be accepted. Permanent and semi-permanent structures such as houses, mobile homes and their associated services such as water mains, sewerage pipes and septic tanks should be located landward of the cyclic erosion envelope. In the progressive case such structures should be

19

Photo 9. Storm damage to 'soft' dune defences at Narin, Co. Donegal. A double row of hay bales had been emplaced seaward of the foredune terrace to protect the primary dune ridge.

located well landward of the projected shoreline position during the expected life of the structure.

If the judgement is that erosion must be halted or slowed down coastal defences can be used. A management guide such as this is not the appropriate place for an in-depth discussion of coastal defence techniques. However some general points can be made: as a matter of policy preference should be given to low cost, environmentally friendly techniques such as sand trapping and stabilising devices, and beach nourishment (see photo 9). A comprehensive account of these "soft" techniques is given in ECOPRO (1996), while those relating specifically to sand dunes are discussed in Brooks (1979). Only in places where it is absolutely unavoidable should engineered defences (concrete seawalls or rock armour) be deployed. An example of such circumstances might be to protect some vital utility or cultural feature that cannot be moved elsewhere. Choice of these engineered "hard" techniques involves considerable administrative and legal complexity and high capital and maintenance costs. Many of these techniques are described in the CERC *Shore Protection Manual* (CERC, 1984) and its successor, the electronically accessible *Coastal Engineering Manual* (CHL, 2000). Beach managers should also be keenly aware of the dangers such hard defences pose for the future and integrity of the beach system. If hard defences are used efforts should be made to use the natural stone of the area rather than concrete, and to tie the structure into the shore so as to prevent accelerated erosion at the ends of the defences.

Issue: Dune erosion and sand blow

Photo 10. Dune blowout at Carrickfin, Co. Donegal. Blowouts can have natural causes and not all are linked to recreational pressure. The ecological health of the dunes is partly dependent on the grazing regime.

Description: Quite apart from storm-wave erosion of the dune front, wind action also erodes sand from exposed dune faces both on the shoreline and further inland in the dunefield. Areas of concentrated deflation become the roughly circular depressions known as blowouts (see photo 10) or more linear deeply etched gullies. Initiation of these features may be either due to natural processes or human activities that result in the localised destruction of the protective dune vegetation, thereby exposing unconsolidated sand to the action of the wind. Among these causes are wave erosion, overgrazing either by rabbits or domestic stock, fires either natural or human in origin, disease, sand pits, and trampling by pedestrians and ATVs. In some areas farmers cut dune vegetation for various purposes e.g. thatching materials. Construction work associated with housing and infrastructural development can also lead to the exposure of dune sand to the wind. Sand blown inland

is a net loss to the beach/dune sediment system while more immediate problems are that sand blow is a nuisance and can adversely affect houses, farm crops and animals and the greens and fairways on golf courses. In the worst case scenario entire buildings and roads can be buried by the relentless landward advance of unanchored dunes.

Response:

Sand blow on the beach is absolutely necessary for dune-building. Consequently any human interference must not obstruct its dune-building function. Contemporary opinion is that a fully vegetated dune system is not desirable. As discussed in section 4.4 grazing both by wild and domesticated animals which produces localised areas of bare sand is now seen as generally beneficial to the biodiversity of dune habitats. For example, burrows create areas of exposed sand which can be colonised by pioneer species and other specialist plants and their associated fauna. However large scale deflation, sand blow and the initiation of blowouts and gullies are not desirable. Various well-tried techniques exist to deal with the problems of wind erosion and deflation (see Brooks 1979 and ECOPRO 1996). Blowouts can be closed with brushwood fences and sand fencing. The exposed slopes of bare sand can be thatched with forestry thinnings or mulch mats and planted with marram or other sand binding grass species. In extreme causes dunes can be rebuilt and re-profiled before thatching and planting. Steep scarp slopes can be protected from the wind with fine fishing net pegged across the dune front (see photo 12). Sand blow onto the back beach area can be lessened by the judicious placing of entrances and access paths and the use of brushwood barriers and sand fences (see photo 11). Beach access points should not run shore normal, and should be designed with a dogleg plan to prevent uninterrupted sand blow. Blowouts and gullies further inland are more difficult to deal with since marram grass planting will not be as successful in the absence of a continuous sand input from the beach.

Photo 11. Netting designed to protect greens from wind-blown sand on Narin-Portnoo Golf Course, Co. Donegal.

Photo 12. Narin, Co. Donegal: Use of a fine shrimp net to protect the golf course from wind-blown sand. The black net is visually obtrusive, but no other colour was available. A seaweed mulch was applied to the exposed sand surface under the net to encourage vegetation growth.

Issue: Sediment starvation

Photo 13. Rock armour revetment emplaced to protect a caravan park at Rossnowlagh, Co. Donegal.

Description: A beach must receive supplies of sand if it is to maintain itself and the dunes. If sand supply diminishes or stops the beach must readjust. A common adjustment is that the beach becomes narrower and steeper and gravel replaces sand as the main component of the sediment. Sediment starvation can result naturally from the depletion of an offshore or alongshore source, but it is often the consequence of human activities. Shore parallel coastal defence structures prevent waves from eroding cliffs and bluffs (see photo 13), while shore normal jetties and groynes prevent sand moving along the shore from areas of net erosion to the beaches where it was formerly deposited. Starved of their sediment supply these beaches erode. Dredging and aggregate extraction offshore can also remove sand deposits which feed nearby beaches, and by deepening the water allow larger more destructive waves to impact the beach. Removal of beach sand by farmers and contractors also contributes to sand depletion. Where rivers contribute most of the sand to nearby beaches the construction of dams upstream can lead to beach loss by preventing sand from reaching the coast.

Response:

Efforts should be made to map the sediment cells along each stretch of coast and in each the source area, transport path and deposition area should be identified. Sediment source areas such as cliffs and bluffs should be allowed to erode and defence structures should only be installed where they are necessary to protect life and substantial property interests. In this context it is obvious that planning control which insists on a prudent set back of coastal development will make it easier to allow cliffs to erode. Similarly it is essential that there should be no obstacles placed in the sand transport path. In Maine USA, for example, groynes are banned by law (Kelley *et al.* 1989). Where groynes and jetties already exist they should be removed if they serve no useful function. If removal is not an option, for example in the case of river mouth jetties, bypassing of sand from one side of the obstacle to the other can be considered. Nourishment of downdrift beaches either from the trapped sand body or from other sources is another possible response. Sand mining from the beach should be banned in all circumstances.

Issue: Flooding

Description: Elevated water levels during storms may inundate low-lying sections of the dunefield. In most cases this is little problem since permanent occupation of these areas is relatively rare, at least in the European setting. However, the flooding problem is a more serious issue in low-lying areas located landward (bayside) of eroding barrier or spit beaches. The danger here lies in the threat that the protective barrier will be breached during a storm leading to inundation of the area to landward. Even without actual breaching storm overwash and the throwing of sediment over the ridge threaten property. Prevention of breaching may be used as a justification for armouring sections of the ocean beach shoreline. Flooding is also a possibility on low-lying land on the landward side of beaches at the mouths of tidal estuaries. The danger in the latter case stems from a combination of high river flood discharge and exteme high tides augmented by storm surge.

Response:

Photo 14. Local people are concerned that shorefront properties at Ballyness Bay, Co. Donegal (foreground) are at risk of flooding if the neck of the Dooey sandspit (centre left) breaches during a storm. (The playing field discussed in case study 7 is arrowed.)

Planning restrictions on development in areas prone to flood risk is the best way of dealing with this problem. In the case of existing settlements, engineers from the relevant local authority should take levels to establish whether the flooding risk is real or perceived. If the risk is real then relocation and compensation may be appropriate responses. The construction of earth or rubble bunds to protect the boundaries of bayside property immediately at risk is a more appropriate response than armouring and fixing a natural sandy shoreline which brings the risks outlined in chapter 2.

Playing field

Issue: Algal bloom (red tide)

Description: An algal bloom (often called a 'red tide' after the colour of one particularly noticeable species) is a largely natural phenomenon, although there may be a contribution from nutrient enrichment due to fertiliser runoff, sewage and excreta from fish-farm cages. Blooms often originate well out in the shelf waters, but prevailing winds may drive them onshore into coastal re-entrants and embayments. The bloom is the result of a temporary very rapid growth of marine algae (phytoplankton) in the surface waters. Rapid proliferation is encouraged by warm seas and high levels of nutrients in the water. As the nutrients become scarce the phase of rapid growth is replaced by massive and sudden mortality. As they decompose the algae consume large quantities of oxygen dissolved in the water, causing the water to become anaerobic. This in turn kills many forms of aquatic life and large quantities of shellfish, worms, sea urchins, flat fish and bottom dwellers are washed up on beaches. In some cases the bloom algae may have a direct highly toxic effect on fish and shellfish, and humans are at risk from eating contaminated shellfish. There is also some health risk from the decomposing organisms on the beach and in the nearshore waters. Additional and immediate problems lie with the appearance of the beach and the smell of decomposing marine life, so it is an aesthetic as well as a public health issue. Algal blooms can sometimes be quite localised with one beach badly affected while nearby beaches have few problems. Others cover large areas and all the beaches are adversely affected. They are unpredictable both temporally and spatially.

Response:

In practice nothing can be done about the algal bloom itself. Normally these events last for just a few days before they break up. Strong offshore winds and rough seas help to expedite this process. In more serious cases the beach should be closed to the public (see case study 2). Such decisions are usually made by local authorities

---

Case Study 2

Algal blooms have occurred in recent years at the Donegal Blue Flag beaches of Rossnowlagh and Downings. In 1997 an algal bloom occurred in Sheephaven Bay with dead shellfish washed up on the beaches at Dunfanaghy and Downings. In the summer of 1999 warm seas off Donegal resulted in a number of outbreaks. The major resort beach of Rossnowlagh in Donegal Bay had to be closed for the three days of the August Bank Holiday weekend. Tonnes of dead shellfish were washed up on the shore, and the smell of decay was so strong that visitors could not approach the beach. Nearby beaches were relatively unaffected. Less intense algal bloom effects littered beaches all around Donegal Bay and Loughros More bay with the remains of thousands of sea urchins. Following these blooms health authorities banned the harvesting and consumption of shellfish until early September. In August 2000 widespread algal bloom effects all along the western seaboard again forced Irish health authorities to temporarily ban shellfish-harvesting in over 30 bays and sea areas.

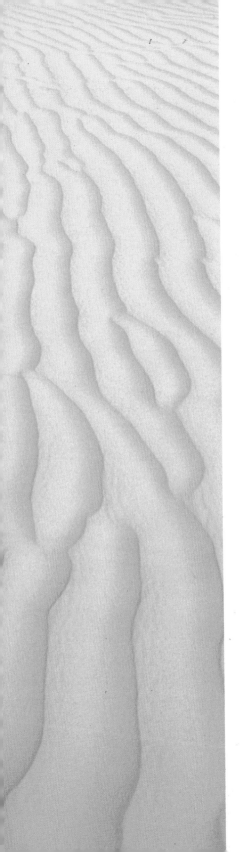

acting on the advice of their water chemists and public health professionals. It is important that beach managers should have an emergency plan to deal with beach closure for this or any other reason (see section 4.3). Signs should be kept in storage and a strategy to effectively close the beach access points should be worked out. It is very important that the signs should give an explanation for the beach closure, as this will greatly encourage public co-operation.

4.2: Issues primarily related to access

Issue: Traffic congestion

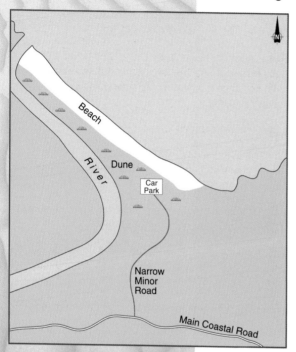

Figure 3. *This schematic diagram illustrates the access problems created by beach location and the limitations of the existing road network.*

Description: Typically rural beaches have a seasonal traffic pattern characterised by very high volumes of traffic on good days during the summer holiday season, and a much lower base volume at other times. Congestion is the inevitable consequence when very large numbers of vehicles converge on the same place at the same time. However, the beach environment has particular characteristics which exacerbate the congestion problem. Beaches by definition lie along a land-sea boundary and, on an idealised landmass, all traffic to and from the site must remain within an approximately 180 degree sector. In reality there is an enormous variety of beach layout and topographic setting, but the broad problem remains that the sea presents a permanent "obstacle" to traffic along one side of the site. In some cases location geometry gives even less freedom of manoeuvre, e.g. beaches located on narrow spits, peninsulas and headlands. In these circumstances the potential traffic sector is often significantly less than 90 degrees (see figure 3).

Control of traffic to beaches is made difficult by a number of additional factors:

(i) The day-to-day unpredictability of the rush to the coast because of daily variations in weather

(ii) The narrow winding roads typical of many rural areas which were not designed to deal with high-volume traffic

(iii) The lack of parking areas near the beach which forces cars to park on the roadside and reduces traffic to single lane

(iv) The concentration of some beach facilities in limited areas, e.g. parking, toilets and lifeguarded zones, which in turn concentrates visitor traffic

(v) The fact that many drivers have only a relatively sketchy knowledge of the road network around the site which leads to wrong turnings, backups etc.

Response:

There is no complete solution to the traffic congestion problem. As noted above the geometry of the site often presents insoluble problems, while authorities, understandably, will not sanction expensive road upgrading schemes for areas where congestion is episodic, generally outside the working week and does not impinge on broader economic and social interests. However, traffic congestion can be eased by a number of strategies:

(a)   Provision of public transport from the largest nearby town. If the service is frequent and the fares competitive many visitors may leave their cars at home to avoid the problems of traffic congestion and parking.

(b)   Provision of off-road parking areas close to or even on the beach.

(c)   Good early signposting of the beach and its facilities plus warnings about restrictions.

(d)   Use of traffic wardens, signs, cones, road markings to prevent roadside parking.

(e)   Introduction of a one-way system in which traffic approaching the beach is separated from traffic leaving (see case study 3).

(f)   The use of beach webcams to provide prior warning of traffic conditions (see case study 4).

Case Study 3

At Rossnowlagh, Co. Donegal a seasonal one-way traffic management system is operated by the local Gardaí (police) in co-operation with the local authority, Donegal County Council. The system, known as ALERT, is initiated on weekends and public holidays during the May-August tourist season on the basis of weather forecast data. When ALERT is in operation traffic must approach the site from the south and leave on the northern side.

Case Study 4

During 1998-1999 at Rossnowlagh, Co. Donegal the LIFE project operated a webcam trained on the beach from an elevated vantage point. Although only experimental it attracted a great deal of interest from the public. On-site a webcam has a potential management use for monitoring general traffic flow and parking. Where beach parking is permitted it allows the manager to monitor vehicle numbers, parking area/tidal stage relationships and driving behaviour. In general a webcam allows the beach manager to assess the spatial and temporal variation in site use throughout the day, and link these changes to weather and tidal variations. Off-site potential visitors can check the traffic and parking situation before they travel. They can also check marine variables; the user group most interested in the Rossnowlagh webcam were surfers as the site is one of Ireland's major surfing beaches.

Issue: Car parking

Photo 15. The car park at Narin Beach, Co. Donegal was constructed over what had been an area of degraded dunes. Beach parking was banned after 1995.

Description: Parking is one of the common problems of beach resorts, including rural sites. Large numbers of visitors arrive on summer weekends and public holidays during spells of good weather. Given the often poor or non-existent public transport in rural areas the vast majority of these visitors will arrive by car. Once at the site the cars must be parked, and for several reasons most visitors want to park their cars as close to the beach as possible. Both very young and elderly visitors cannot be expected to walk long distances from car to beach. Some visitors, especially older people, prefer to stay close to the comfort and shelter of their cars but with a good view of the seascape, while parents want to keep their children on the beach in view. The car is often used as a base for the visit, serving variously as changing room, wind-break, and entertainment centre with access to refreshments and music.

This demand for parking provision very close to the beach access points can often bring problems (see photo 15). Such points are often located in sensitive dune areas where habitat loss due to car park construction, and the degradation generated by the concentration of pedestrians, may be undesirable. Other problems derive from the siting of other visitor facilities in or close to the car parks, e.g. toilets and fast food outlets, leading to litter and waste disposal problems. If land adjacent to the beach is privately owned, purchase of the relatively large tracts of land needed for car parks may be prohibitively expensive or impossible. In any case the cost-effectiveness of large permanent car parks at rural beaches may be questioned if maximum visitor volumes are reached only a few times per year.

Response:

Development plans for recreational beaches in rural areas should include parking provision near the beach. However, it should be recognised that a rural beach cannot be expected to provide a place in a permanent car park for every vehicle that arrives on the busiest day of the year. Some ideas to ease parking problems and their associated side effects are:

(i)   With the co-operation of the landowners, provide temporary car parks on busy days.

(ii)   Where possible locate car parks on mineral soil or bedrock rather than in sand dunes. The temptation to use sand dunes is strong because it is much easier and cheaper to level land where the substrate is unconsolidated. Nevertheless environmental considerations should have priority.

(iii) Car parks are best located at the extremities of a beach rather than in the centre. The beach margins are more likely to have areas of mineral soil or rock (see above) while central locations will usually have dunes at risk from visitor pressure. Beach margins are also more likely than beach centre locations to have elevated positions with unobstructed views, suitable both for appreciating scenery and supervising children.

(iv) Wherever the car park is located avoid constructing shore-parallel feeder roads as these tend to be used as linear car parks (see photo 16). Roadside parking leads to environmental damage as visitors cross the intervening dunes to the beach. If shore-parallel roads cannot be avoided position them well back (at least 200-300m) from the beach and provide substantial fencing. Discourage parking by making the roads no wider than necessary for two vehicles to pass.

(v) Provide large car park(s) on mineral soil on the periphery of the site with a shuttle bus service to the beach.

(vi) Give preferential treatment to buses and coaches by reserving for them the most convenient parking places close to the beach. This may encourage visitors to use these means of transport and cut down on the total number of vehicles.

(vii) Provide several small car parks rather than one large one. This will help to spread traffic and visitor pressure more evenly over the resort. In some cases it may be environmentally more acceptable to concentrate the pressure on only a few points which are explicitly managed to sustain that pressure.

(viii) Provide directions to alternative nearby beaches.

(ix) As a last resort consider parking on the beach (see below).

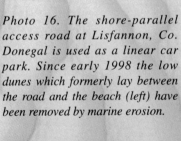

Photo 16. The shore-parallel access road at Lisfannon, Co. Donegal is used as a linear car park. Since early 1998 the low dunes which formerly lay between the road and the beach (left) have been removed by marine erosion.

Issue: Beach parking

Photo 17. In July 2000 uncontrolled beach driving and parking at Rossnowlagh, Co. Donegal led to the suspension of the resort's Blue Flag award. On the bottom left the erratic course of a quad bike can be followed from its tracks.

Description: On a number of beaches there is a tradition of beach parking (see photo 17 and case study 5). At some sites there is no charge while at others there is a flat rate charge per vehicle. At the National Trust site of Portstewart Strand, Co. Derry N. Ireland there can be up to 1,500 cars parked on the beach on a sunny summer Sunday. Currently each car is charged £2.50 sterling. There are obvious benefits from beach parking in that it helps to alleviate traffic congestion and parking problems on the approach roads (although high tides can force cars back off the beach). The income generated from charges can be used to pay for other management initiatives. Many visitors value beach parking because it is the ultimate realisation of their desire to get their cars as close to the beach as possible for the reasons listed above. There is also a sense that beach parking may be environmentally acceptable because high tides quickly remove all traces of driving activity, giving the impression that the beach is self-cleansing.

Unfortunately beach parking brings problems. As yet there is no unequivocal evidence that it is damaging beaches, but some coastal scientists believe that compaction of the sand by vehicles may lead to accelerated erosion by reducing the percolation of outgoing backwash. Beach fauna is usually impoverished on such beaches and this may also be linked to compaction. Beach traffic undoubtedly compromises visitor safety. The absence of road markings and signs along with the general lack of police monitoring often encourage irresponsible driving, especially by young men. This is added to by the perception, often wrong, that road traffic laws do not apply on a beach. The risk to other beach-users, especially children, is heightened because they are in a relaxed recreational environment where normal traffic awareness and vigilance may be dulled. The driving problem is particularly serious

Case Study 5

In Co. Donegal beach parking is, or has been, allowed at several Blue Flag beaches. At Narin in west Donegal the practice was discontinued after 1995. There have been no complaints and the off-beach car parks are at full capacity on only a few days per year. At Downings in north Donegal the whole beach was formerly available for parking but since 1997 part of the beach is car-free. Moves to make the entire beach car-free are hindered by the lack of off-beach parking capacity and the limitations of the narrow local roads. At the larger resort of Rossnowlagh in south Donegal the beach is still a free car park and thoroughfare used by thousands of vehicles on busy days. The beach has three uncontrolled access points which connect directly to the road network. Local people, especially farmers, value the beach thoroughfare as a convenient shortcut. Every year there are serious concerns expressed over beach safety, and several cases of dangerous driving reach the local courts.

where the beach has no vehicle access control and has more than one vehicle entrance. In these circumstances the beach becomes not only a car park but a thoroughfare forming part of a circuit linked to the local road system. As well as posing a risk, vehicles can cause noise, nuisance and lower the recreational and scenic quality of the site for beach users.

Response:

Safety and environmental concerns, and the requirement of the European Blue Flag scheme that at least part of a beach must be car-free, have led to a decline in beach parking. The practice is no longer permitted at several sites that used to allow it (see case study 5). There remain a few locations where the loss of beach parking might create serious congestion problems and bring a risk of total traffic chaos leading to gridlock. At these sites off-beach parking is simply not available and the narrow local roads cannot handle holiday traffic volumes. In these circumstances the best that can be achieved may be that the greater part of the beach remains car-free while one section is designated for parking. If only part of a beach is car-free then the barrier on the beach should extend seawards far enough to prevent motorists from driving around the seaward end to reach the car-free zone. Bollards should be spaced to present an effective barrier to vehicles. It would be prudent for a beach management authority to consider its legal liability before continuing beach parking. This is especially important if charges are made.

Issue: Environmental damage caused by vehicles

Description: Apart from the total loss of dune habitat due to car park and access road construction, and the potential environmental damage caused by beach parking and driving, vehicles can cause damage to a site if they are allowed to drive or park on the dunes. The fragile dune vegetation and unconsolidated sand substrate have a very limited load bearing capacity, and deep ruts quickly appear. As the ruts deepen drivers move laterally onto undamaged dune to avoid grounding the cross members of their vehicles. Thus the rutted degraded area quickly increases in size (see photo 18). The bare sand exposed in this way is vulnerable to wind erosion and the rutted area can become a major deflation blowout. (The problems caused by the recreational use of ATVs and scrambling motorcycles are dealt with in section 4.3.)

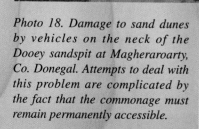

Photo 18. Damage to sand dunes by vehicles on the neck of the Dooey sandspit at Magheraroarty, Co. Donegal. Attempts to deal with this problem are complicated by the fact that the commonage must remain permanently accessible.

Response:

The only areas where driving or parking should be permitted are those explicitly designated for that purpose. Informal "customary" car parking areas should be strongly discouraged. This will be easier to achieve if adequate formal parking is available. Perimeter fences or hedges should be used to confine vehicles to the designated areas. If vehicles must be routed across an area of dune it is not always necessary to provide a hard-core or tarmac surface. Railway sleepers or similar wooden beams can provide a firm base without the permanence of an engineered roadway. Pedestrian access points can be incorporated in the fences. If a continuous fence is deemed inappropriate, e.g. where pedestrians need to be able to cross a traffic control barrier all along its length, lines of bollards can replace the fence. It is particularly important that individual bollards are spaced so that they are an effective barrier to vehicles. Signs can be used to explain why the dunes must be protected. Once protective fencing is in place areas of dune already damaged should be restored using some of the techniques described in Brooks (1979) and ECOPRO (1996). Again the opportunity should be taken to educate the public about this work with informative signs.

Issue: Environmental damage caused by trampling.

Description: At most sites this is a more serious problem than that caused by vehicles. Cars are relatively easy to control but pedestrians can go almost anywhere, are less predictable and many of them are younger people who are less amenable to regimentation than the average motorist. In practice pedestrians do little harm to the beach itself, but they can do a considerable amount of damage to sand dunes. The main reason for this is that they trample the dune vegetation along the myriad of paths that tend to develop on busy visitor sites. The main species present in European dune systems is marram grass (*Ammophila arenaria*). Marram is a tough species with remarkable adaptations to its harsh sand dune environment, but its Achilles heel is its vulnerability to trampling. It is important to point out, however, that the aim of most dune conservation/ecosystem management is not to maintain a fully vegetated dune system. Contemporary opinion is that a degree of disturbance that creates limited areas of bare sand is beneficial to the ecology of sand dune systems. This is because biodiversity is increased as specialised or opportunistic species colonise the bare sand. Even paths can contribute to this process, but the problem lies in the scale of path erosion.

Photo 19. Trampling damage to vegetation on the frontal dune ridge at Culdaff, Co. Donegal. If pedestrians continue to use this route the path could one day become a gully or possibly a substantial blowout.

Photo 20. A dune-front boardwalk at the National Trust beach at Cushendun, Co. Antrim. The boardwalk is part of a rehabilitation scheme for the site that also includes sand fencing and re-profiling dunes.

Trampling of dune vegetation occurs mainly because pedestrians tend to take the shortest route to the beach that is physically passable. For energetic young people the threshold of what is passable is quite high. If car parks, access roads, caravan sites or other facilities lie immediately landward of the beach, visitors will create paths as they traverse the dunes (see photo 19). A dune crest path is also typical as visitors on the beach use the frontal ridge as a vantage point. Children often slide down the face of the frontal dune. As the paths develop, vegetation dies back and areas of bare sand are created. Strong winds, and in the case of frontal dunes, storm waves, can attack the areas of exposed loose sand. The paths erode into gullies and, in time, the gullies may develop into substantial blowouts where the entire vegetation cover has been destroyed.

Response:

Pedestrians do not usually intend to cause damage to dunes. They are simply moving to and from the beach. Since, in practice, most paths lead from access points or recreational facilities one way to minimise path creation is to locate these on mineral soil or bedrock at the extremities of the beach. A concentration of beach facilities would also help to reduce the number of paths required. If pedestrian traffic must cross the dunes management strategies should take advantage of the fact that most visitors tend to take the line of least resistance. This means that, if a path is provided, they will tend to use it. Beach managers should provide a limited number of clearly marked boardwalk paths with even (but not smooth) surfaces, and wide enough to walk two abreast (see photo 20). If possible at least some of the paths should permit disabled access. The paths should be dog-legged as they traverse the frontal dune ridge to prevent sand blown from the beach being funnelled landward. Elsewhere, shore parallel fencing should be substantial enough to dissuade visitors from crossing the dunes. The fences flanking the designated route across the dunes need not be high and can even be set some distance back from the boardwalk. In summary the relatively simple stratagem of providing a few formal and convenient routes (with surfaces that are easier to walk on than dune vegetation) can prevent the creation of many informal paths. Again damaged areas should be restored as noted above.

Issue: Public access to the beach

Photo 21. Sign warning the public not to trespass on privately owned dunes at Rossnowlagh, Co. Donegal.

Description: This is a vexed issue in many rural areas. The idea that the general public has a right of access to the seashore is very old and is associated with traditional economic activities such as shooting, fishing, shellfish harvesting, bait gathering, beachcombing, and the harvesting of marram grass and seaweed. Even though most of these activities have declined or ceased, the perception of the shore as a common resource for all people is deeply rooted, and the protection of access for recreation and enjoyment of nature has become an important aim for sections of the environmental movement. Many traditional routes to the shore cross privately owned land and have acquired the status of rights of way. Some of these have legal protection (termed a "public" right of way in UK and Irish law) and the right of way is marked on deed maps. Not all mapped rights of way can be used by the general public; some are specific to certain householders only. The other broad group consists of customary rights of way (termed "permissive" or "permissible" rights of way in Britain and Ireland), i.e. routes across private land used with the owner's permission. Most of these rights of way are unmapped and were established many years ago as verbal agreements between the owner and habitual users of the route.

Today rights of way are generally under threat and particularly so in the coastal zone. As coastal property become increasingly sought after and therefore more valuable, a tendency to seek exclusive use of the shorefront manifests itself. The result of this trend is that members of the public are often denied access to the shore across private property (see photo 21). This has generated many bitter conflicts, some of which have led to litigation. In many jurisdictions the inter-tidal beach is usually owned by the State (Republic of Ireland, UK) but public ownership of the beach itself does not resolve the access problem where the supra-tidal land is privately owned. Most at risk are routes where the existing right of way is conditional on the owner's permission without any other explicit legal basis (see case study 6). As property changes hands a new owner may be unwilling to allow the right of way. Even where public access is not explicitly banned there may be a strong "chill factor" that dissuades people from crossing certain properties to reach the beach. For example, a golf club occupying an extensive stretch of coastal land will often discourage the public from crossing the course, usually stating safety concerns. Visitors are forced to use beach access points at the margins of the course, leading to environmental degradation of these over-used areas.

Case Study 6

In Co. Mayo, Ireland there is a long-running controversy over access to Uggool beach at the mouth of Killary Harbour. Before 1989 the beach had been part of a popular hiking trail linking the coast with the mountains inland, but after that date the landowner prevented public access by erecting fencing. This led to public protests. In 1997 the local authority Mayo County Council stated that, because the beach had been fenced off for five years, it was prevented from taking any action to restore access. However it pledged to acquire a new public right of way under the Planning Acts. However this action is greatly complicated by the fact that the Council must first ascertain the identity of some 200 registered owners of commonage over which the right of way would extend. The issue is not a simple farmer versus public situation. Many local farmers are fully in support of the landowner, and have protested publicly on his behalf. An additional factor in this local dispute may be the current contention between Irish farming organisations and the Government over their public liability if members of the public are injured crossing their lands.

Response:

Control of access is crucial to effective beach and dune management. It can be used to restrict or enhance levels of use and is therefore imperative in any management plan. On public property where access points already exist roads, car parks and paths should be well maintained and clearly signposted. The access needs of disabled visitors should also be accommodated. Given the modern tendency to litigation it is important to give careful attention to public safety and public liability issues. Any attempt by landowners of private property to block access routes to the shore along a public right of way should be strongly resisted. Elsewhere, however, access restrictions can be introduced with the co-operation of landowners within the context of an agreed management strategy.

Government agencies, local authorities and conservation NGOs should be acutely aware of the importance of maintaining rights of way as a means of ensuring that the public can have access to the shore. Where a public (i.e. with legal status) or permissible (i.e. customary) right of way does not exist, and access is clearly required, authorities should endeavour to negotiate an access agreement with the landowner. Statutory authorities could negotiate such access agreements directly, or indirectly by providing funding for NGOs like The National Trust in the UK which has successfully negotiated many such agreements. The main element of these agreements is that a landowner cedes the use of a narrow strip of land a few metres wide, parallel to the shore, along with a routeway to the coastal road. Occasionally the landowner may also be prepared to cede ground for a small car park. On these strips of land waymarked paths are constructed. Landowners gain in that they will suffer much less from illegal and occasionally damaging trespass on their lands. They also gain new fences on the seaward side of their properties constructed and maintained at the expense of the local authority, statutory conservation body or NGO. This can

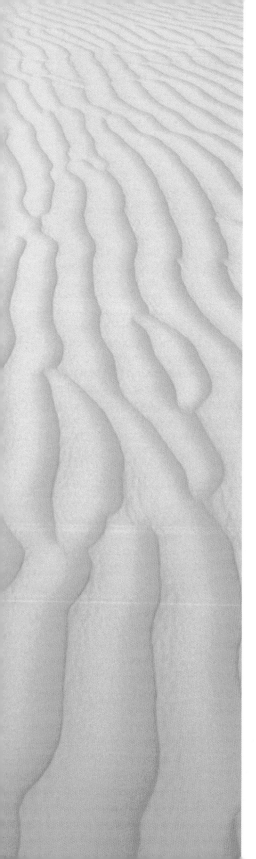

be a useful bonus on an eroding coast. The public gains the access it wants without the risks and inconvenience of crossing fences and difficult wet terrain. Another advantage of negotiated access agreements is that landowners, who would strongly resist any demand for a public right of way, may be quite willing to negotiate access agreements.

Clearly the longer the time period covered by an access agreement the better. However, all voluntary agreements run the risk of termination, especially when property changes hands. For this reason at important access routes to a popular beach authorities should either negotiate a public right of way or an outright purchase of the access route. In a few cases where agreement cannot be reached, and where there is no feasible alternative, the authority should consider imposing a compulsory public right of way or even compulsory purchase of the access route. These negotiated or compulsory options should also be considered where an existing and heavily used right of way is permissible rather than public. Because of the expense and time involved in legal process and compensation the compulsory options should only be used as a last resort and where usage of the route is heavy enough to justify such extreme measures. Beach management authorities also need to be aware that in some countries an existing right of way can become lost if not used. This is more likely to occur nowadays than in the past because many visitors and even locals are unaware that the right of way exists. This may mean that a formal exercise of right of way needs to be carried out and documented.

4.3 Issues primarily related to recreational use

Issue: Beach and water user conflicts

Description: Beaches are adaptable areas that can be put to a wide variety of uses. Not all of these uses are compatible and, when incompatible uses take place in proximity, conflicts can occur. Uses can be incompatible for a number of reasons. Some are simply mutually exclusive, for instance an area of dune cannot be a football pitch and a tarmac car park at the same time. Likewise, bird watching cannot be pursued in an area where people are engaged in dune buggy scrambling. Some uses are incompatible because they produce unacceptable levels of risk, e.g. jetskiing and swimming, or nuisance, e.g. sports training and sunbathing. Finally, certain activities can lead to a loss of amenity, e.g. inappropriate housing development can diminish the visual enjoyment of a landscape. Table 3 illustrates the possible compatibility of some common activities. For example, the shaded column indicates the possible compatibility of sunbathing with some other activities. In practice, the compatibility of activities will vary from site to site. Some of these incompatibilities are subjective, and whether or not they are considered problematic will depend on factors such as the individual's risk perception or noise tolerance. Differences of opinion should therefore be expected when attempting to manage potentially incompatible activities.

Table 3. A compatibility matrix showing examples of possible conflicts on beaches.

Compatibility Matrix for Beach Use

Examples of possible conflicts on beaches:

OK	Compatible
X	mutually exclusive
!	potential risk
✱	nuisance
▲	loss of amenity
?	unknown

	Jetskiing	Swimming	Sunbathing	Car driving	Aquaculture (on the foreshore)	Birdwatching (in the dunes)	Caravan park	Football pitch	Sports training
Swimming	!								
Sunbathing	OK ✱	OK							
Car driving	OK	OK	! ✱						
Aquaculture (on the foreshore)	✱	✱	OK	✱					
Birdwatching (in the dunes)	✱ ▲	OK	?	✱ ▲	OK ?				
Caravan park	OK	OK	OK	!	▲	▲ ?			
Football pitch	OK	OK	OK ✱ ?	OK ?	OK	▲	✱ X ?		
Sports training	OK ?	OK	✱	✱ ?	OK	▲	✱ X	OK	

The aim should be to manage conflicting activities in ways that enable them to co-exist harmoniously. If this cannot be achieved then efforts should be made to enable them to at least exist with acceptable levels of risk, nuisance and loss of amenity. If the means of allowing activities to co-exist cannot be found then a decision has to be made regarding which activities should be removed from the site. This decision should take into account the wishes of beach users and residents and the inconvenience and loss of amenity caused by the removal of an activity.

Response:

Banning an activity altogether is an extreme step and should only be used as a last resort. Although it may sometimes be necessary, monitoring and enforcing a ban can be very difficult, particularly in more remote areas. A ban that is ignored can create

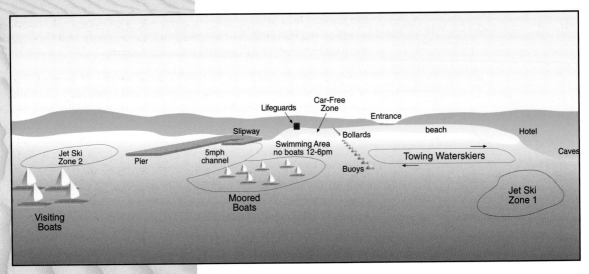

Figure 4. The zoning scheme at Downings, Co. Donegal.

contempt for those failing to enforce it, and prove counterproductive. Even if enforcement is successful it may simply lead to the displacement of the problem, rather than its solution.

Zoning activities is generally preferable to banning them as it enables activities to co-exist. Activities can be zoned temporally or spatially, i.e. they can be restricted to certain times or areas, or both. The zoning scheme devised by the boat club at Downings, Co Donegal (see figure 4) is an example of a scheme that restricts activities both spatially and temporally. Cars are not allowed into the area of the beach marked out with bollards at any time, and boats and jetskis are not allowed inside the swimming zone marked out with buoys between 12.00 and 18.00. Zoning schemes can also be applied at certain times of year, usually when the site is likely to be busiest.

Banning or zoning activities requires the provision of information, in the form of signs, notices etc., outlining where, when, why and by whom the activities are being restricted. They also require clear demarcation such as fencing, bollards and buoys. Monitoring and enforcement is also important and, depending on the site, can be carried out by officials such as the police, lifeguards or beach wardens. In some cases it may be possible to have a self-policing scheme or to leave enforcement up to the local community. Attempts should be made to consult with the local community before putting any of these in place.

Issue: Health and safety at the beach

Description: There are many potential threats to safety and public health in the beach environment. This is inevitable when there are many different activities taking place in a restricted, and often crowded, area. The presence of water and young children add to the threats. In addition, there is often less regulation of activities, whether recreational or industrial, in coastal areas and this can increase the level of risk posed by various hazards.

The hazards at a beach can come from a variety of sources (see table 4). They can be the result of: natural processes (e.g. tides and currents, rockfalls, algal blooms, jellyfish, razor shells and sea urchins, decomposing marine life); incompatible activities taking place in proximity (e.g. jetskiing and swimming, or car driving and sunbathing); inappropriate activities or inadequate management (e.g. water quality problems, inadequate signage); users' behaviour (e.g. recklessness, thoughtless behaviour, ignorance of the potential hazards). Some hazards are the result of a combination of the above. For instance, broken glass could be regarded as the result of thoughtless behaviour, or of inappropriate management, or a mixture of the two depending on the circumstances.

Table 4. Examples illustrating the range of hazards at rural beaches and possible management responses.

Cause of the hazard	Example	Reducing the source of the hazard	Isolating the source of the hazard
Natural processes	Falling rocks	Slope stabilisation.	Fencing off areas, warning signs.
	Dangerous shellfish	Removal of hazardous material.	Warning signs.
	Currents, waves or tides		Warning signs.
	Storms	Storm defences, building design etc.	Set back lines, evacuation.
	Rotting carcasses	Removing or burying carcasses.	Fencing off areas, warning signs.
	Algal blooms	(Preventative action if cause is anthropogenic.)	System for preventing access during emergencies.
Incompatible activities	Jetskis and swimmers	Speed limits, training, licensing and codes of conduct for jetskiers, bans.	Zoning activities, controlling access.
	Cars and pedestrians	Speed limits, codes of conduct, enforcing traffic laws, bans.	Zoning activities, controlling access.
	Horses and pedestrians	Codes of conduct, limiting numbers, bans.	Zoning activities, controlling access.
Inappropriate activities/ inadequate management	Poor water quality	Identify the cause(s) and reduce or treat.	Close beach, fence off areas, warning signs.
	Illegal rubbish dumping	Organise clean ups, enforce dumping bans.	Provide facilities and areas for dumping.
	Washed up hazardous material, e.g. phosphorous flares, mines, chemical spills, WWII shells.	(Preventative action if possible.)	Isolate hazard and inform the emergency services. Warning signs if a frequent occurrence. System for preventing access.
	Falling from pier or harbour wall	Provide safety rails. Codes of conduct and speed limits in harbours.	Control access to the danger area.
Users' behaviour	Reckless driving	Passing and enforcing legislation, community action, calming measures such as bollards.	Encourage the use of designated areas, formal zoning.
	Swimming in dangerous water	Discourage use of the area - use signs, alert lifeguards.	Control access.
	Littering	Beach clean ups, enforcing littering bans, signs and education, provide bins.	Try to limit the problem to certain areas, e.g. put picnic areas next to car parks.

Response:

The specific response depends on the nature of the hazard. Individual hazards such as jetskiing or uncontrolled dogs are dealt with in detail under separate headings. The overall aim of those engaged in beach management should be to minimise the risks to beach users' health and safety. This involves carrying out an audit to identify the potential hazards, assessing the risks and then devising a plan to manage them (see Kay and Alder 1999, p196-201). There are many books that look at the theory of safety (e.g. Stranks 1997) and organisations such as the Royal Society for the Prevention of Accidents (UK) or the National Safety Council (Ireland) can provide guidance on specific issues. If the level of risk posed by a hazard is considered unacceptable then, in broad terms, one can either seek to (a) reduce the danger in some way, (b) deal with the consequences of the danger, or (c) attempt some combination of the two. In order to reduce the danger one can either reduce the source of the danger or try to stop people coming into contact with the danger. For example, if there was a danger of rockfall then a slope could either be stabilised to reduce the number of falling stones or an area could be fenced off to stop people entering the danger zone. Table 4 gives some more examples of ways of reducing danger. Dealing with the consequences of the danger involves accepting the current level of risk and concentrating on remedial measures that either reduce the consequences (e.g. provision of lifeguards, life saving equipment, ambulance access points and qualified first aiders), or transfer the consequences (e.g. insurance, disaster relief schemes).

Finally, anyone planning to become involved in the management of safety issues should bear in mind that not all hazards are visible or predictable. It is therefore important to be methodical and thorough when managing potential hazards. It is also important to be aware of the responsibility involved and the possibility of legal liability. The legal position regarding any initiatives should be clarified before being implemented.

Issue: Bathing water quality

Description: Rural beaches are often in areas where there is either no mains sewerage or where the existing system is old and designed for small resident populations. In the worst cases completely untreated raw sewage, or partially treated (i.e. primary treatment only) sewage, is released into the sea near beaches. In addition streams flowing into the sea across or close to beaches are sometimes contaminated with agricultural effluents from slurry or silage. There can also be natural threats to water quality, e.g. algal blooms (see section 4.1). Even where a mains sewerage scheme does exist the huge expansion of caravan parks and holiday homes plus daytripper populations often means that it cannot cope and is overloaded. Surprisingly planning authorities often allow new holiday home and caravan park developments in coastal areas where the existing sewerage schemes are clearly inadequate.

In areas without a mains sewer system individual septic tanks are normally used. These do not always function efficiently and problems with smell and leaking effluents can occur. If the effluents flow directly into the sea or a coastal stream they can contaminate bathing waters. Tanks associated with caravan parks and holiday homes located in sand dunes can cause local saturation of the sand, leading to nutrient enrichment which encourages the growth of plant species not normally found in the dune environment. Recently there has been a trend towards the use of sealed septic tank systems which do not allow interaction with the surrounding soil. In these cases the residue is removed by tankers at intervals. Some areas have installed group sewerage schemes that represent an intermediate stage between individual tanks and a fully integrated mains system.

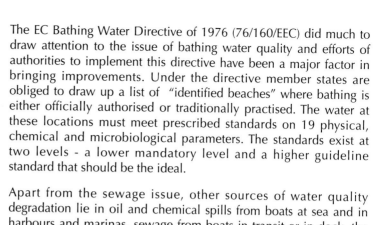

The EC Bathing Water Directive of 1976 (76/160/EEC) did much to draw attention to the issue of bathing water quality and efforts of authorities to implement this directive have been a major factor in bringing improvements. Under the directive member states are obliged to draw up a list of "identified beaches" where bathing is either officially authorised or traditionally practised. The water at these locations must meet prescribed standards on 19 physical, chemical and microbiological parameters. The standards exist at two levels - a lower mandatory level and a higher guideline standard that should be the ideal.

Apart from the sewage issue, other sources of water quality degradation lie in oil and chemical spills from boats at sea and in harbours and marinas, sewage from boats in transit or in dock, the effects of anti-fouling paints and fish waste from fishing boats or dockside handling.

Response:

Beach users should not be overly fastidious. The smell of sea and seaweed and a degree of natural organic decomposition are perfectly natural parts of the beach environment and should not be confused with water pollution. There are no quick fixes for water quality problems where the only solution lies in the installation of a modern mains sewerage system or at least the upgrading of an existing one. The capital costs of such schemes are very high, lead-in times are long, and there may also be some reluctance to install new schemes where the permanent resident population is low. Therefore it is probably unrealistic to expect that all rural beaches will ever be linked to mains schemes. The development of group schemes and the installation of more efficient sealed individual tanks would appear to offer the best way forward. Recently there has been a welcome trend where planning authorities require developers to provide, or contribute to, a new or improved waste disposal system. Local sources of point pollution can of course be tackled, e.g. farmers washing slurry tankers in coastal streams inland from the beach. Faulty individual systems can also be identified and the owners obliged to deal with the problem.

Recreational awards such as the FEEE Blue Flag scheme help to focus attention on the water quality issue because they demand sampling and attainment of Directive standards. Recent changes to the Blue Flag regulations have widened their scope to include streams flowing on or near the designated beach. It is possible that at some sites authorities may be persuaded to fast-track sewage treatment schemes to gain or preserve a high status recreational designation. Oil, chemical and fish waste pollution can be dealt with by the introduction and enforcement of suitable handling and storage regulations.

Issue: Fast powered water craft

Description: Fast powered water craft, essentially speedboats and jetskis, are a common feature of rural beaches, particularly on the busier, resort type beaches. They are likely to increase in usage in the future as levels of disposable income increase. A great deal of concern has been expressed recently about the hazard that jetskis can pose, as the headlines in figure 5 show. Some of these fears were confirmed in 1999 when a young jetskier was killed in County Sligo, Ireland, after colliding with a boat.

Figure 5. Headlines illustrating the recent controversy that jetskis have attracted in Ireland.

Although both speedboats and jetskis present similar potential problems (i.e. noise pollution, nuisance and danger), in practice they present different management issues. One of the differences is in the type of people that use them. Speedboats tend to be owned by the user, who will therefore have a certain amount of experience. Jetskis, by contrast, are often hired and are more likely to be used by the young and/or inexperienced. It could be argued that jetskis pose a greater threat to the safety of other water users because they are more likely to be used in a reckless or unskilled way. In addition jetskis tend to be used nearer the shore than speedboats because of their shallower draft and the user's wish to be seen by other beach users. They are therefore more likely to come into contact with bathers.

Response:

There are a number of ways in which the risk posed by these craft can be reduced. Speed limits, codes of conduct, training, licensing and awareness raising can all help. Those hiring out jetskis to the public can be encouraged to take some responsibility for their customers. However, the nature of these craft means that many people find the level of risk and noise produced by them intolerable on some beaches. In such circumstances it may be necessary to zone or ban them (see figure 4). Their use can be limited to designated areas of the beach, or allowed only at certain times of day or during certain periods. Areas can be marked out with buoys to make them unambiguous. It should be remembered that zoning on its own may not be enough, as jetskis and speedboats can pose a threat to each other if used improperly. Remedial measures such as lifeguards, first aid and compulsory insurance for craft users may prove useful should an accident occur.

Jetskis and speedboats often require different management responses. In particular, jetski usage is more difficult to control and this presents certain challenges. Once in the water, it is difficult to prevent a jetski from being used inappropriately. If misuse is a persistent problem, then action should be taken to control launching. As jetskis can be launched from the beach, preventing cars from getting onto a beach is one way of controlling them. Use of piers, slipways and harbours can also be controlled. If someone is determined to gain access to a particular area of water then it is very difficult to prevent this. However, the vehicle used for transporting the craft can be located and the details passed on to the appropriate authorities.

Issue: Dog control

Description: Dog walking is a common activity on many rural beaches. It takes place all year round, unlike more weather-dependent or seasonal activities. Problems are more likely to occur during the summer months when the dog walkers share the beach with many other users and large numbers of young children. While many people like dogs, they can also produce a range of negative reactions in beach users from mild annoyance to terror. In extreme circumstances they can cause injury if not properly controlled, and can pose a serious threat to other animals such as sheep. Dog fouling is also a common problem. It is unsightly, offensive and poses a health hazard, especially to young children.

Response:

If uncontrolled dogs are a problem on a beach then signs should be erected establishing a code of conduct, and dog owners should be educated and encouraged to act responsibly. Off-leash zones can be established if necessary, outside which dogs must be kept on a leash. If children's play areas exist then dogs should not be allowed near these under any circumstances. If a dune system is grazed by sheep then dogs should be kept on the leash. Dog fouling can be reduced by providing dedicated dog waste bins and "pooper-scoopers". Alternatively, a degraded area of dune can be set aside as a dog-fouling area. If measures are persistently ignored and dogs are spoiling visitors' enjoyment of an area then dog wardens may have to be employed to ensure that measures are observed.

Issue: Horses

Description: The presence of horses on beaches poses different problems to dogs. They are generally less common than dogs, less likely to be uncontrolled and their droppings do not represent a health hazard. Individual horses, therefore, rarely cause any serious problems. Action may be required if a beach is small, or particularly busy, or if it attracts large numbers of horses, for instance if it is near to a riding school.

Response:

Codes of conduct and signs can be used if horses are being ridden in ways that cause annoyance or danger. They can also be restricted to certain areas of the beach or to certain times of day. Given the large amount of space required to exercise a horse, temporal zoning may be preferable to spatial zoning. Horses can be allowed unlimited access to the beach when it is quiet, i.e. early in the morning and in the evening, in return for being banned during the rest of the day. Outside the summer season, it may be possible to allow horses unlimited access to the beach.

Issue: Litter and beach cleaning

Description: Most beach visitors will have encountered the problem of litter and rubbish. It is a widespread and persistent problem that affects most public spaces to some degree. Some litter is dropped by careless or thoughtless visitors, while other litter is washed in by the waves or blown in by the wind. Its main impact is visual, although some material, such as broken bottles, also poses a health risk. The severity of the problem varies from beach to beach, and depends on factors such as the number of visitors, their attitudes, and the management regime in place. On some beaches litter is a problem for a short period during the peak season. On others it is a problem all year round. Litter is an immediately visible problem and one that is high on the list of most people's complaints. It is therefore one that should be given a high priority as, rightly or wrongly, it influences visitors' perceptions of a beach and of the way in which it is managed.

Response:

Two approaches can be employed: (a) litter can be prevented from appearing on the site, and; (b) the litter that does appear can be removed. In practice a combination of these approaches will usually be required. Litter can be prevented from appearing by encouraging people, e.g. through the use of signs, to dispose of litter properly. Litter wardens and fines can be used to persuade those who remain otherwise unconvinced. Providing easily identified and accessed bins is also important. Bins should be large and should be emptied often. The number and location of bins should reflect the patterns of littering on a site. Unfortunately some individuals use bins as an opportunity to dump material that should be disposed of in other ways. However, it is still important to provide bins as their absence gives people an excuse to drop litter, and makes it more difficult to encourage responsible attitudes. Specially designed bins can help to prevent them being used for domestic or commercial dumping. In addition, the provision of facilities for the disposal of material that should not be put in bins (e.g. domestic waste from caravans), should help to prevent dumping.

Removing litter is expensive and it could be argued that it is wrong in principle for people to expect others to clean up their mess. Ideally individuals should take responsibility for their own actions. However littering, like other forms of anti-social behaviour, reflects larger social problems that are beyond the scope of beach management to tackle. It is often necessary to be pragmatic and deal with the consequences, particularly as not all litter is deposited deliberately - some is washed in, blown in or left accidentally. People can be paid to collect litter or volunteers can be encouraged to take part. Facilities (e.g. gloves and bags) and support such as transportation should be provided for volunteers by the appropriate

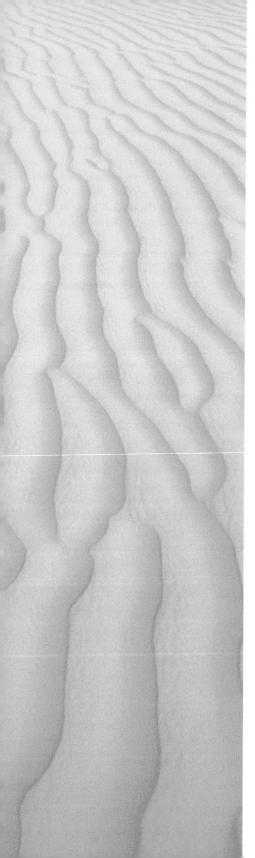

authority. Using volunteer schemes has the advantage that it engenders a sense of ownership of the beach that is useful in management.

Mechanical cleaning, for instance employing a tractor and harrow, should be avoided where possible as the removal of large amounts of seaweed can damage a beach. As discussed in section 4.4 seaweed helps to trap sand and build dunes (see photo 28). It also plays an important role in beach ecology, as the invertebrates that live in it provide food for bird populations. The criteria for Blue Flag beaches state that "No algal or other vegetation may accumulate and be left to decay on the beach, except in areas designated for a specific use" (see the Blue Flag guidelines at http://www.blueflag.org). However this ignores the role that seaweed plays in the beach system (see Royal Society for the Protection of Birds 1998, "Red Card for Blue Flags?", in *Sixth Sense* the RSPB magazine). Instead of mechanical cleaning the litter that accumulates in the seaweed can be removed by hand. If the presence of the seaweed itself is considered intolerable then it can be removed from the busiest part of the beach but left in place elsewhere.

The design of a site can affect the amount of litter present. If litter is concentrated in certain areas such as car parks, picnic areas, and shops it makes collection easier. Efforts should be made to identify features that attract litter and locate these close to each other. Those with commercial interests in a site should be encouraged to help prevent litter by taking responsibility for the area surrounding their premises. Activities that produce unacceptable levels of litter, such as raves or illegal camping, should be identified and either prevented or managed. Overall, the litter management strategy should take into account the changing needs of the beach. Some beaches require year round cleaning, while others only need to be cleaned during the peak season. Occasional one-off clean-ups may be required after certain events such as storms or busy public holidays. It is often worth having a major clean-up just before the peak season starts, especially on beaches that are cleaned infrequently during the off-peak season.

In the UK the Marine Conservation Society carries out an annual environmental campaign called Beachwatch. This takes the form of a beach litter survey and clean-up carried out every September involving thousands of volunteers. The results of the survey are published in a Beachwatch report. Developed from the Beachwatch campaign is a UK-wide Adopt-a-Beach scheme which co-ordinates volunteers in carrying out regular surveys and beach cleans of local coastal stretches. In Ireland an annual litter survey has been carried out since 1987 by volunteers acting for the Irish branch of the Coastwatch Europe Network. The Coastwatch survey also collates information on a wide range of issues including coastal erosion.

Issue: Public toilets

Description: Many visitors spend several hours at a time on a beach so there is often a demand for some form of toilet facilities. The absence of toilets can cause inconvenience to the visitor and also to the proprietors of nearby pubs and shops to which people turn in their moment of need. However, public toilets are expensive to install and maintain, and can have adverse effects on the water quality or scenic character of a site. The decision whether or not to provide public toilets is therefore one that requires careful consideration of all the costs and benefits. It will depend in part on the character of a beach and the number and types of visitors it attracts. For example, toilets are less important on quiet beaches or those where people only stay for an hour or two, and more important on beaches that attract a lot of young children (it should be borne in mind that the lack of toilets may be a reason why visitors leave after relatively short periods of time).

Response:

If it is decided that the benefits of toilets outweigh the costs, then a number of secondary decisions have to be made: What type and size of toilets are required - is a permanent block required or should portable units be put in place for the peak season only? (portable units are cheaper but present access problems for the disabled); How many should there be?; Where should they be? (they need to be conveniently situated and easily located, without spoiling the scenic quality); When should they be open?; When should they be cleaned?; Who is responsible for their maintenance? As this list of questions shows, toilets involve a considerable commitment of time and money. Some of the expense can be recouped by charging a small fee for the use of the toilets. This has the added advantage of discouraging vandalism. Another strategy for reducing the burden is to share the responsibility for the toilets between different bodies, e.g. a local authority may be able to come to some arrangement with another body who stand to gain from them such as a harbour authority, café, or sports club.

Issue: Use of all terrain vehicles (ATVs)/Dune scrambling

Description: Dune systems, while resilient, are susceptible to erosion from off-road vehicles such as quads, dune buggies and trail bikes. These vehicles can lead to gullying, blowouts and general dune degradation (see photo 22). In addition to the physical damage, scrambling produces levels of noise, danger and nuisance that are unacceptable to many beach users. There can also be a loss of amenity as few activities are compatible with scrambling, for instance birdwatching or sunbathing cannot take place in the same area as scrambling.

Response:

The problem can be avoided through the provision of alternative facilities for scrambling away from the beach. For instance if there is some waste ground available nearby then scramblers could be encouraged to use it. This will not always be an option and in some cases it may be that beaches are used because they are the only suitable land in the vicinity. It may be necessary to ban scrambling and prevent off-road vehicles from gaining access to the site (see section 4.2). However the nature of these vehicles makes it difficult to stop the determined person gaining access, so there may be a need for some way of removing those that do gain access. This should not be left to the lifeguards who should be concentrating on the water and are usually only present for the summer months. If there are beach wardens then they should prevent scrambling when they are present. If there is no warden then a combination of beach users, the local community and the police should attempt to control scrambling. Any initiatives to ban or control scrambling should be accompanied by activities to make scramblers aware of the reasons underlying the initiatives. If it proves impossible to prevent scrambling then it may be necessary to manage it in ways that minimise its impact. An area could be set aside for scrambling, preferably on degraded inland dunes away from the main recreational parts of the site. The area should be fenced off and have notices explaining the conditions of usage. This should be a last resort as the creation of such an area may attract more scrambling and exacerbate the problem; continuing efforts should be made to find a non-coastal site for scrambling.

Photo 22. Recent tracks produced by a quad or similar off-road vehicle at Lisfannon, Co. Donegal.

48

Issue: Anti-social behaviour

Description: Anti-social behaviour at beaches can take many forms. These range from trivial acts such as dropping litter to potentially life-threatening behaviour like reckless driving or vandalism of safety equipment. In this guide, anti-social behaviour is defined as any actions that cause any significant annoyance or risk to other people. Box 2 lists activities that could be deemed anti-social in some way. Quite often it is the way in which an activity is carried out that makes it problematic, rather than the activity *per se*. Although these actions differ in seriousness, they are all activities that can needlessly reduce other people's enjoyment of the beach, and as such they should not be tolerated if they are being carried out in an anti-social manner.

Box 2. Some of the many activities that could be deemed anti-social in certain circumstances.

...causing a nuisance...acting in a disorderly manner...swearing or behaving indecently...causing danger or obstruction...consuming controlled substances...drinking alcohol...throwing stones...having a dog not under proper control...damaging dunes, fences etc...marking trees, structures etc...lighting fires...possessing firearms...interfering with safety equipment or notices...setting off fireworks...depositing refuse or litter...burying animals...bringing on horses or other animals...bringing on vehicles...using fast power craft...criminal activity such as theft...

Response:

There is an element of subjectivity in deciding what is dangerous or annoying, and consequently what constitutes anti-social behaviour. Some people do not find jetskiing annoying while others do (see figure 5). In cases where there are differences of opinion, consensus should be determined. When an activity is agreed to be undesirable then action should be taken to stop it. Who should take responsibility for this depends on what is happening, and where and when it is taking place. Other beach users, lifeguards, wardens, local communities, police, local authorities, relatives and proprietors of amenities may all have to take action. Ultimately the responsibility lies with those that are behaving in the undesirable way to change their behaviour once they are made aware that their actions are unacceptable. Sometimes technical solutions to problems such as vandalism can be helpful. Toilets and other facilities can be locked or designed to discourage such behaviour. However these are only part of the solution as those determined to cause damage will often find some way to do so. In some cases technical solutions may merely act as a challenge. If certain types of behaviour are persistent problems then the causes need to be identified. The causes will often involve factors that are beyond the influence of beach management, for instance there is nothing that a beach manager can do about the social background of the visitor. However, if factors such as alcohol or boredom are thought to be contributing, then attempts could be made to tackle these. Rossnowlagh in Co. Donegal suffers from persistent vandalism and disruptive behaviour caused by adolescents. It is believed that this is

49

linked to the fact that a lot of families spend long periods (2-6 weeks) on the site during the summer and there are limited facilities to occupy the youths. In such circumstances providing appropriate leisure facilities could help to alleviate the problem. A pragmatic approach to controlling anti-social behaviour is required as there are rarely any easy or complete solutions. Failure to realise this could lead to unrealistic expectations and disappointment. Awareness raising of those engaged in anti-social behaviour should be central to any strategy, although expecting education to act as a panacea is unrealistic.

Issue: Sports facilities in dune systems

Description: Dune systems in rural areas often contain sports facilities such as football pitches or golf courses (see case study 7 and the discussion on tenure in section 4.5). There are several reasons for this. Dune systems tend to be well drained and, in some countries such as Scotland and Ireland, often have extensive flat areas that are rare in the surrounding countryside. Those that do not possess flat areas are easier to level than other types of land, an important factor in hilly coastal areas. In agricultural terms dune systems are less adaptable and therefore less valuable than other types of land. In addition, dune topography lends itself well to golf, and coastal "links" sites are prized. The presence of sports facilities can have a number of impacts on a dune system. Any feature that attracts large numbers has the potential to cause trampling, dune degradation, litter and the other problems associated with the presence of significant numbers of people. They also affect the natural integrity of the site and can reduce its scenic quality and biodiversity. Some sports grasslands require high levels of maintenance and the use of large amounts of fertiliser and water.

Case Study 7

In many parts of Ireland the only suitable sites (relatively flat, well-drained, but non-agricultural land) for playing fields are located on the margins of coastal dunes or machair. Of the seven sites in the Co. Donegal LIFE Project five have, or once had, a football field on part of the site. One of these is at Magheraroarty in north Donegal where for many years there has been a soccer field on the neck of the Dooey Peninsula sandspit, a jointly owned commonage (see photo 14 in section 4.1). The local football club upgraded the previously informal playing field in 1997, and imported soil to top-dress the surface. The spit is part of a cSAC and unsurprisingly Dúchas, Ireland's national conservation agency, has expressed concern about this clear example of a damaging operation inside a statutorily protected area. However, the political reality is that local opinion is so heavily in favour of the playing field development that Dúchas is left in a difficult position in its efforts to redress the situation. Tellingly the football club was much more concerned about local sensibilities than about national or EC legislation. Thus the club, which consulted no one about spreading topsoil on the playing field, went to the considerable trouble of asking permission from every joint owner of the spit before fencing the new field. The first action was not an issue for local people, but the second was potentially contentious because it could be construed as an attempt to claim ownership of part of the commonage.

Response:

Sports facilities tend to reduce biodiversity, scenic quality, and can lead to the degradation of the site. However rural areas often suffer from social problems such as outmigration and unemployment and playing fields and golf courses can bring money into areas and provide much-needed amenities for locals. A balance needs to be struck between the exploitation and conservation of dune systems. As a general principle any development should be sustainable - there is no point exploiting a site for short-term gain, whether financial or political. Sometimes it may be unacceptable to develop sports facilities, for instance if an area has been designated a SAC or is of high scenic quality. Careful consideration should be given to the need for a facility, not just its desirability or commercial viability. For instance, the number of golf courses in Europe has nearly doubled (98% increase) in the last 15 years. This may lead some to express doubts regarding the need for more courses, particularly in a country like France that has seen the number of courses more than double (an increase of 228% in the last 15 years, figures quoted are from the European Golf Association, http://www.ega-golf.ch/pages/statistic.html).

If sports facilities are to exist in dune systems then they should be designed and managed in ways that minimise their impact. Schemes such as "Committed to Green" (http://www.committedtogreen.org/) can provide advice on ways of achieving this. Attention should be paid to issues such as access, parking and movement, the use of pesticides and fertilisers, location and scenic quality, water quality and litter.

Issue: Children's play areas

Description: Beaches are popular places for parents to take children. There can be large numbers of young children present when the weather is good, especially during the school holidays. Play areas with facilities such as swings and climbing frames can be a useful addition to the site (see photo 23), providing a safe and enjoyable facility for children. They can act as a focus of activity away from more sensitive beach areas and can attract particular types of visitors to a site. Play areas will not be appropriate at all beaches, and will generally be better suited to the busier, amenity-type beaches.

Photo 23. A play area in the dunes at Culdaff, Co. Donegal.

Response:

If it is felt that a play area is desirable, then the costs and benefits of creating and maintaining it should be calculated so that an informed decision can be made. If the decision is positive then a range of

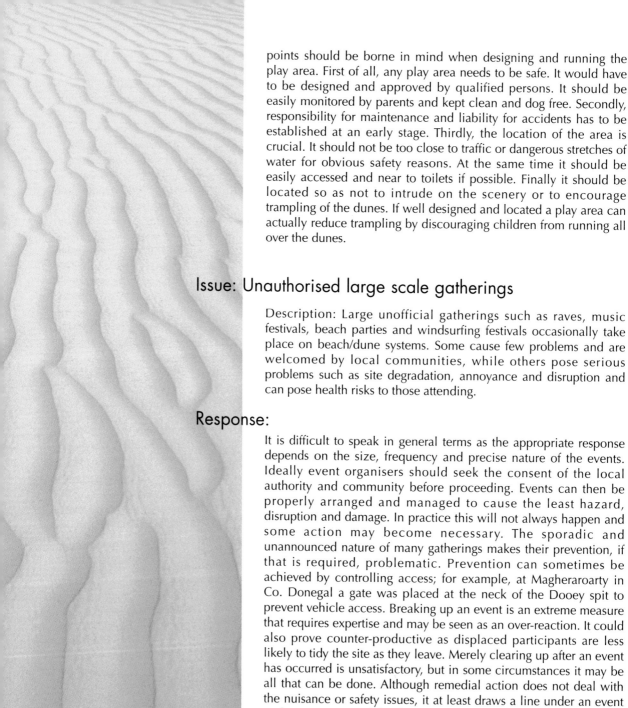

points should be borne in mind when designing and running the play area. First of all, any play area needs to be safe. It would have to be designed and approved by qualified persons. It should be easily monitored by parents and kept clean and dog free. Secondly, responsibility for maintenance and liability for accidents has to be established at an early stage. Thirdly, the location of the area is crucial. It should not be too close to traffic or dangerous stretches of water for obvious safety reasons. At the same time it should be easily accessed and near to toilets if possible. Finally it should be located so as not to intrude on the scenery or to encourage trampling of the dunes. If well designed and located a play area can actually reduce trampling by discouraging children from running all over the dunes.

Issue: Unauthorised large scale gatherings

Description: Large unofficial gatherings such as raves, music festivals, beach parties and windsurfing festivals occasionally take place on beach/dune systems. Some cause few problems and are welcomed by local communities, while others pose serious problems such as site degradation, annoyance and disruption and can pose health risks to those attending.

Response:

It is difficult to speak in general terms as the appropriate response depends on the size, frequency and precise nature of the events. Ideally event organisers should seek the consent of the local authority and community before proceeding. Events can then be properly arranged and managed to cause the least hazard, disruption and damage. In practice this will not always happen and some action may become necessary. The sporadic and unannounced nature of many gatherings makes their prevention, if that is required, problematic. Prevention can sometimes be achieved by controlling access; for example, at Magheraroarty in Co. Donegal a gate was placed at the neck of the Dooey spit to prevent vehicle access. Breaking up an event is an extreme measure that requires expertise and may be seen as an over-reaction. It could also prove counter-productive as displaced participants are less likely to tidy the site as they leave. Merely clearing up after an event has occurred is unsatisfactory, but in some circumstances it may be all that can be done. Although remedial action does not deal with the nuisance or safety issues, it at least draws a line under an event and restores some of the damage caused.

4.4: Issues primarily related to non-recreational use

Issue: Sand mining from beach and dunes

Description: At many rural beaches there is a long established practice of sand removal for a variety of purposes. These include the bedding of animals, the sanding of muddied field entrances and yards, improvement of heavy or acid soils, golf course maintenance and general construction. The practice was often quite sophisticated, e.g. leached dune sand with its lower lime content was preferred for building, with carbonate-rich beach sand used for neutralising acid soils. Gravel storm ridges lying landward of the sand beaches were also extensively mined for aggregate and drainage stones. The perception developed that the beach was a public resource with locals having the right to use its sediment in much the same way as they might gather seaweed or harvest dune grass. Over time these traditional practices attained the status of "prescriptive" rights, and in the British Isles in some cases they have legal protection under Common Law. Until the early part of the 20th century technology set limits on the amount of sand that could be removed - for example shovels and horse carts could only remove limited amounts. However, as technology advanced the introduction of excavators, front-loading tractors, heavy steel trailers and lorries made it possible to remove very large quantities (see photos 24 and 25). On some beaches commercial sand extraction operations were established, e.g. this practice continued at Portrush, Co. Antrim in Northern Ireland until 1973.

Photo 24. Sand mining from dunes on the northern margin of the River Erne estuary, Co. Donegal.

Photo 25. Sand mining inside a cSAC, Port Arthur, Co.Donegal, August 2000.

Large scale sand removal over a long period gives rise to serious problems. In many locations the sediment losses simply exacerbate an existing condition of sand scarcity - the normal natural state of many beaches in Europe today. Beach sand is a finite resource. Most beaches consist of a relatively thin lens of sand that quickly wedges out a short distance offshore. Frequently there is no contemporary source of sand, as many of today's beaches are composed of glacial sediments sorted and moved onshore by rising sea levels at the end of the last glaciation. On a compartmentalised coast where bay-head beaches lie between prominent headlands there is little or no potential for fresh sand input to the beach from alongshore. Since the position and form of a beach is a balance between incoming wave energy and sediment availability any significant diminution in the latter will tend to lead to profile readjustment. This readjustment often takes the form of beach narrrowing and steepening leading to enhanced shoreline erosion.

Generally the practice of large-scale sand mining on beaches has declined. Increased environmental awareness and changes in farming practices have been the main factors in this decline. In most jurisdictions it is now banned by law or bye-law, but enforcement is a problem in rural areas, and there are few beaches where sand mining does not occur from time to time.

Response:

Where the practice of beach sand mining is illegal the problem is solely one of enforcement. Beach signs and occasional media exposure should make it clear to the public that the practice is both illegal and harmful. A study of sand mining in Northern Ireland (Carter *et al.* 1992) indicated that increased public awareness of its damaging environmental consequences had played a significant role in its decline. It was noted that those involved now operated on days and at times where they were less likely to encounter other beach users. They also preferred to use a secondary beach access where one existed, rather than use the main entrance. Members of the public were more prepared to challenge offenders, note vehicle numbers and report them to the authorities. The lesson here is that public information and education can be powerful tools in eliminating this insidious practice. Beach managers should photograph and record evidence of ongoing or recent activity. Secondary beach access points used by the sand miners should be blocked off with substantial fences or bollards. Authorities should not overreact, e.g. against someone taking a small quantity of sand for garden use, but the threat of litigation against persistent offenders should be real. However, both statutory bodies and environmental NGOs are often reluctant to instigate proceedings against members of a farming community whose co-operation they need in other areas.

The problem is more intractable where there is a legal right (or an arguable case that there is a legal right) to remove beach sand. Courts tend to be reluctant to interfere with such rights. In this case the beach manager must patiently liaise with the local community with the aim of achieving voluntary reduction or elimination of the practice (see case study 8). Public education on the harmful effects of sand mining should underpin these efforts.

Issue: Channel dredging and offshore aggregate extraction

Description: Dredging is an increasingly common practice. As well as maintenance dredging of existing waterways, navigation channels must be deepened and widened as vessels grow in size. The contemporary expansion of water-based recreation has also seen a boom in marina construction with the associated dredging of basins and channels. In many areas sources of aggregate on land are getting scarce, and the construction and quarrying industries are looking at the exploitation of marine sources. Removal of the sand shoals themselves represents a loss of habitat, while other potential problems result from the release of large quantities of fine grained sediment which is harmful to marine life and incompatible with water-based recreation. There are also other, less obvious, consequences of dredging. Sand shoals frequently form part of an integrated sediment circulation system that links the frontal dunes, the inter-tidal beach and the sub-tidal inshore zone. There are few if any inputs or outputs - the sand moves around within a basically closed system. The situation is particularly sensitive on beaches near estuary or other river inlets where the sand shoals are intimately linked with the other elements to cycle sand around and through the inlet, e.g. the Tuns Bank, off Magilligan foreland, in Co. Derry Northern Ireland, forms part of a sand transport and storage system which also includes the recreational beach at Benone on the northern flank of the foreland. The removal of sand from sub-tidal shoals and bars represents a net loss to the sediment system, and if the scale of sand removal is above a threshold the morphology will readjust to the loss of volume. These adjustments can be difficult to predict. Dredging deepens the water thus allowing larger waves to break closer to the shore, thereby enhancing erosion and threatening property. Increased water depths may also change wave-breaking characteristics so that in some places wave focussing leads to enhanced erosion while in other locations unwelcome deposition may begin. Deepening estuarine channels also allows salt water to penetrate further upstream which can cause ecological stress and contaminate public water supply intakes.

Response:

Navigational dredging and aggregate extraction are not usually beach management issues where they take place well away from the shore and there are no potential knock-on effects. However, many recreational beaches have an estuary mouth location and lie close to navigation channels, while new marinas too often lie adjacent to sand beaches. Response to problems associated with dredging can be problematic because dredging is an expensive operation usually commissioned by government agencies or large companies such as port authorities. These bodies tend to be powerful, and can marshall strong economic arguments to justify dredging which often outweigh recreational or conservation considerations. Indeed there are situations when the statutory agency which commissions dredging is also responsible for monitoring its environmental consequences! In most European jurisdictions Environmental Impact Statements are required, although the demands of the EIS could often be a lot more rigorous, e.g. it should be compulsory to undertake wave refraction modelling to estimate changes in erosion and deposition patterns consequent on dredging. One potential benefit of dredging is that the dredged material may be available for beach nourishment provided that the sediment characteristics are close to those of the natural beach. Those charged with managing beaches should monitor closely any proposed dredging activities and, if there are fears that the beach might be affected, representations should be made to the appropriate authority.

Issue: Undergrazing and overgrazing

Description: Dune grasslands have traditionally played an important role for livestock grazing systems in coastal areas. Their long-term use as pasture and rabbit warrens is commonly recorded in historical texts and on old maps. Dune systems also support significant populations of wild grazing animals, including invertebrates, birds and mammals.

Grazing pressure is usually focussed on the mature dune habitats (e.g. grey dune, machair plain and associated wetlands). These are more productive than marram-dominated mobile and semi-fixed dunes, and contain a greater proportion of palatable vegetation. They contain the largest number of species on the dune system, and have great visual appeal owing to the abundance of flowers, birds, butterflies and other invertebrates present throughout the summer months. Grazing maintains these habitats in their typical form by

Photo 26. Overgrazed dune pasture on the Dooey Peninsula at Magheraroarty, Co. Donegal. Other characteristic problems of open-access commonage are illustrated by the presence of litter, campfire debris, and a burned-out car.

the selective removal of a proportion of the annual standing crop (biomass). Selective grazing behaviour encourages vegetation diversity as some plants are favoured and others are avoided (see photo 27). Grazing also helps to redistribute nutrients and seeds around the dune system. In the absence of grazing, coarse grasses, shrubs and eventually trees may invade and become dominant.

In recent years, and perhaps also in former times, it has been relatively easy to find examples of dune systems where the balance between ecological succession, vegetation productivity, soil stability and grazing pressure has been upset (see photo 26). At one end of the spectrum are dune grasslands and machair that have been so heavily grazed that their surface vegetation is damaged, the soil surface becomes unstable and erosion ensues. Several machair systems on the west coast of Ireland have experienced erosion so severe that bedrock below the dune is exposed. Other inappropriate farming practices include: soil enrichment caused by the application of fertiliser and slurry on dunes; sward damage caused by over-wintering of large numbers of livestock on dune pasture; and sand removal for land improvement and building work elsewhere on the holding.

At the other extreme, long term abandonment of grazing management, often coupled with dramatic crashes in the rabbit

Photo 27. Selective grazing at Mullaghmore, Co. Sligo has resulted in the dominance of yellow-flowered ragwort (Senecio jacobaea) in the sward. Ragwort is unpalatable to sheep and poisonous to cattle.

population, has led to the spread of tall competitive grasses and shrubs, and has reduced the area of shorter, open turf on many systems. Abandonment of grazing is perhaps more common in the UK than in Ireland, owing to the acquisition of large areas of coastal land by bodies such as The National Trust.

Response:

It has been a common misconception, at least in Ireland, that curtailing agricultural uses on dune systems is beneficial for nature conservation (see case study 9). Properly managed livestock systems can bring important gains for the conservation value of dune systems. It can be generally assumed that one of the primary goals of a dune manager is to maximise the variety of habitats and species on the site (maximise site biodiversity). Grazing is a valuable tool to achieve this aim. It also can reduce the risk of grass fires.

When planning a grazing system, ecological factors to consider include climate, soils and topography, the initial condition and the desired state of the vegetation. Management factors include the grazing period, grazing intensity and animal type. Practical considerations include the availability of suitable livestock, the market for rented grazing land, agricultural support schemes, condition of fencing, supply of fresh drinking water, monitoring

Case Study 9

In the mid 1960s the sand dunes at Culdaff in northeast Co. Donegal, previously privately owned by a single landowner, were acquired by the local authority Donegal County Council. The high conservation interest of the site is acknowledged by its inclusion in the North Inishowen Coast cSAC. There are aspects of Culdaff's management which are clearly a function of its tenure type. Under private ownership up to 1966 the unfenced dunes were grazed lightly. After that date, and now under public ownership, the dunes were fenced and were quite intensively grazed under lease to the former owner in winter up to the late 1970s. After 1980 the dunes were not grazed at all. It is most unlikely that privately owned dunes, or dunes held jointly, would have remained ungrazed for such a long period. Culdaff then is a relatively rare example of natural dune succession allowed to operate. Local people have seen the end of grazing as a considerable success in their desire for environmental improvement, but a controlled grazing regime is actually beneficial in that it aids biodiversity and prevents the ranker vegetation and scrub from becoming dominant. At Culdaff extensive areas of the dune interior are now covered with a rank vegetation of thick matted grass with bracken and dense thickets of scrub on the landward areas. Grazing was restarted in 1999 on the advice of the national conservation body Dúchas, but a lack of consultation with the local community prompted dissent.

resources and public access requirements. The resultant system will be a compromise between ideal ecological requirements, management factors and practical issues. It is not possible to define an ideal grazing system applicable to all dune systems. A National Trust booklet (Oates *et al.* 1998) describes a large number of case studies that attempted to design and modify grazing systems for dune sites in the UK. As a general rule, sustainable grazing intensities for natural pasture such as dune grassland tend to be much lower than normal agricultural levels, e.g. at or below 0.5 livestock units/ha. Stocking rates should be maintained below the level that causes significant disturbance to the soil surface.

Grazing carried out to reduce the dominance of grasses or shrubs is most effective during the growing season, whereas grazing carried out for site maintenance is most effective if carried out in winter (October-March) to allow flowering and seed set during the summer. Other factors may come into play; for example the presence of important populations of ground-nesting birds means spring grazing is not appropriate. Cattle are often preferred to sheep as their grazing behaviour is less selective, and they allow opportunities for a greater range of species. Sheep prefer short, fine swards to coarser herbage, and therefore often avoid species the manager is attempting to control. Cattle, however, can easily damage wetter and less stable sites, and have more exacting animal husbandry requirements. Though characteristic of many dune systems, rabbits experience huge population fluctuations and are therefore difficult to manage as a grazing animal. Mowing can be considered on a small scale where grazing is not practical or desirable. However, mowing machines do not replicate the action of the grazing animal, such as the creation of regeneration sites in hoof marks; spreading of nutrients and seeds in urine and faeces; and selective browsing leading to habitat patchiness and increased biodiversity.

While it is important to maintain 'open' dune communities and maximise site biodiversity, it must be recognised that this intervention is not natural. In a coastal area where grazing is widespread, it may be of value at some sites to allow natural processes of succession (including fires) to proceed.

Issue: Burning of marram grass

Description: The practice of burning or "firing" marram grass to promote fresh growth of herbage or the spread of more palatable grasses has been reported by several rural communities in the west of Ireland. It is not clear whether this activity is still practised today. The effect of burning live marram will depend on the position of the marram stand within the dune system. If immature marram on unstable or semi-fixed sand is burned, it will not lead to rapid new growth, but will release large amounts of sediment for aeolian transport. Blowouts and widespread erosion, followed by a slow recovery period, are likely consequences of a large fire on the seaward part of a dune system. Fires in the interior of dune systems are less damaging to the integrity of the system. A feature of most natural grassland systems, fires may in one sense be considered beneficial, as invading trees and shrubs may be suppressed. However, deliberate firing of old, moribund stands of marram grass in stable dune grassland will also burn fescue-dominated grassland. Uncontrolled high temperature grass fires may ignite the surface mat and soil layers. Again, surface instability and sand blow may result, removing the organic rich soil and exposing raw dune sand. The fire may also spread to the frontal ridges. The burned areas of the interior may accumulate less desirable, opportunistic species that exploit post-fire environments, such as rosebay willowherb (*Chamaenerion augustifolium*).

Response:

Though part of the natural succession on dune systems, deliberate burning of marram is, at best, of negligible value from an agricultural perspective, and at worst, can lead to undesired instability of large parts of the system. Since livestock farming is being extensified by means of EU subsidies, attempts to increase production from dune swards by burning cannot be justified. More suitable restoration management techniques for undergrazed dunes include grazing and cutting. In summary, the burning of marram grass as a pasture improvement practice is probably not an issue today. However, uncontrolled fires, whether they are started accidentally or maliciously, are of concern to the dune manager.

Issue: Harvesting of marram grass

Description: Marram grass was formerly cut on a large scale on many Irish dune systems for use as animal feed and bedding, and as a makeshift thatching material. A 1954 aerial photograph of the Dooey Peninsula in northwest Donegal shows the geometric patterns of an extensive network of marram cutting bays and associated access roads. These are clearly causing dune instability and initiating blowout formation. Going further back in time, an extensive tract of land on the eastern shore of Sheephaven Bay, including the village of Rosapenna, was inundated in the late 18th century by a sand blow that was the result of excessive marram harvesting on the nearby dunes (Quinn, 1977). Marram harvesting still takes place in Co. Donegal, but on a very small scale.

Response:

It is probably not necessary to restate the negative aspects of clear-cut marram harvesting. While collection of small amounts of marram for traditional thatching projects or for dune restoration is acceptable, large-scale marram harvesting cannot be sustained. At present, no action is necessary as harvesting is not practised on a significant scale.

Issue: Removal of seaweed from beaches

Description: Winter storms and wave action deposit detached seaweed, plant and animal remains, and debris on beaches. This material accumulates as a driftline above the high water mark (see photo 28). In this position, it makes a fundamental contribution to the development and maintenance of the dune system. Firstly, it forms a physical obstruction, leading to accumulation of blowing sand around drift material. Secondly, drift contains seeds of many seashore plants, the majority of which are annuals. These germinate in the growth medium provided by the driftline. It contains nutrients from rotting organic matter and salt spray, and also provides moisture and shelter from the exposed fluctuating environment of the open sandy beach. As the growing season progresses, it may be colonised by sand-binding grasses such as sand couch (*Elymus farctus*) and sand sedge (*Carex arenaria*) that spread seawards from older embryo dunes further up the beach. Animal species, such as sand hoppers and sanderling, will also exploit the strandline. If the strandline survives the storms of the following winter, it may be further colonised by marram, and will begin to grow vertically into a foredune ridge. If it fails to survive, it will have played an important defensive function in protecting the interior dunes from attack. Plant remains, seeds and organic matter released by erosion may end up back in the driftline in the following spring.

Photo 28. The beach at Narin, Co. Donegal with the drift lines of seaweed which are an important part of the dune-building process.

Many beach management authorities currently remove seaweed and other debris from the beach following storms as part of their cleaning programme. They are required to do this under European Blue Flag and UK Seaside Award regulations.

Response:

Action is required to educate the public and beach management authorities of the importance of driftline seaweed for the dune ecosystem. Suitable beach signage plus a newspaper/TV campaign is needed to persuade people that a beach with seaweed is a healthy beach. It is important that foreign objects, such as plastic bottles, animal carcasses and other refuse are manually removed from the driftline during beach cleaning. Where rotting seaweed results in a serious odour problem, removal may ultimately be required. Innovative solutions perhaps involving storage or maceration of the driftline, followed by redistribution, may be required.

Issue: Alien/invasive species

Photo 29. Introduced sea buckthorn on the crest of the primary dune ridge at Narin, Co. Donegal. Terrestrial weeds, derived from hay bales and/or fill used as coastal defences, grow on the foredune terrace to seaward.

Description: Occasionally either naturally, accidentally or deliberately, non-dune plant species are introduced into dune systems. Some are able to survive in dune habitats, whereas others colonise introduced soil and waste (see photo 29). Accidental introductions can take place as species spread from nearby gardens or cultivated areas; in other cases they originate in fill, rubble or garden waste dumped in the dunes. The garden plant montbretia (Crocosmia, x crocosmiiflora), found in several Donegal dune systems, probably gained its foothold as a "garden escape" or where local people dumped garden waste. However, introduction of alien species is often deliberate. Corsican pine (Pinus nigra ssp. laricio) was planted extensively on the Ainesdale dunes of the Sefton coast in eastern England as a commercial forestry operation. In Ireland the shrub, sea buckthorn (Hippophae rhamnoides) was introduced to several sites to stabilise sand, provide windbreaks, and/or to control pedestrian access. Examples are at Downings and Narin in County Donegal, and Portstewart in County Derry. The problems created by these exotic species are twofold. Firstly, the plants are inappropriate in a dune environment, and secondly they may be aggressively invasive and hence can pose a threat to the native flora and fauna of the system (Bingelli et al. 1992).

63

In the British Isles the thorny shrub sea buckthorn (<u>Hippophae rhamnoides</u>) is native only in the coastal region of eastern England, but it has been introduced widely to sand dunes elsewhere for dune stabilisation and pedestrian control. At Portstewart, Co. Derry N. Ireland sea buckthorn was introduced in the 1930s to deter pedestrian access to the sand dunes. By 1989 it had spread vegetatively to cover 13% of the dune area and now forms large stands of impenetrable thickets. The owners of the dune field, The National Trust and the Portstewart Golf Club, are facing problems because sea buckthorn is aggressively invasive and is difficult to control and eradicate. It also leads to a decrease in plant species-richness, displaces botanically uncommon plants and leads to soil enrichment. In the mid-1990s the Trust began a scheme to control the shrub by cutting down and spraying a percentage of the cover. Sea buckthorn does have some beneficial effects, e.g. it stabilises sand, and provides food and habitats for fauna. For this reason the Trust does not intend to eliminate it entirely – the aim is solely to control its distribution.

Response:

The beach manager should follow the precautionary principle on this issue, particularly where the introduced species is known to have an invasive character. Control of dumping will do much to lessen the risk. Conservation designations, particularly those with real power such as SAC, can be used to prevent both dumping and deliberate introductions. On non-designated private lands the situation is more difficult. Landowners who are considering the use of exotic species for management purposes should be apprised of the risks and informed of safer alternatives.

Once they are established control of invasive exotic species can be difficult and expensive. However, there are examples where site managers are trying to restore sand dune habitat on areas now dominated by exotic species. At Portstewart stands of mature sea buckthorn are being cut down (see case study 10), while on the Sefton coast large sections of pine are being clear-felled (Sturgess, 1993). A complicating factor is that the alien species may provide valuable habitat, e.g. the pine-felling programme at Sefton has met opposition from local activists who wish to preserve squirrel habitat.

Issue: Dumping of rubble and fill

Description: Rubble may be dumped just to get rid of it or, less frequently, as an attempt to strengthen and build up an eroding shoreline. Rubble is sometimes used to build and extend terraces that are then used to carry tourist infrastructure such as caravan parks and car parks (see photo 30). Rural beaches are particularly prone to dumping, especially out of season where there are few witnesses around who might create a fuss (see case study 11). Control is very difficult given that some beaches are very large with

Photo 30. A recently extended terrace constructed of imported fill at Downings, Co. Donegal. The terrace allows seaward expansion of the shorefront caravan park.

multiple access points. Where the person responsible owns the dunes it is virtually impossible to control dumping even if it is technically illegal. Fly-tipping of builders' rubble and soil from the excavation of house foundations takes place frequently in the dune interior and along the dune scarp. The situation is greatly aggravated by the absence of convenient formal dumps, and has become especially bad in recent years as many local authorities introduced charges for previously free dumping services.

Arguments that dumping is a contribution to coastal defence do not stand up. Such loose unconsolidated material can make no contribution to preventing or slowing erosion. The material often presents a danger to beach users because nails and pieces of sharp scrap metal are often included. It is unsightly as unvegetated piles of debris with obviously anomalous profiles are scattered over the dunes. The dumping of fill will occasionally introduce a nutrient-rich substrate and the seeds of exotic species (see above), leading to the development of a vegetation complex inappropriate to the beach/dune environment. If the clay content of the fill is high the surface may be sealed leading to waterlogging of the naturally highly permeable sand substrate. If the clay fill is dumped on the beach scarp in wet weather it becomes an unpleasant sticky mat.

Response:

Probably the best action that could be taken is to provide a formal dump somewhere in the locality. Local authorities should seriously reconsider their policy of charging for dumping at these sites. The lesser of two evils is to forego the revenue if the public can be

---

Case Study 11

Dumping of rubble and fill is a common problem on Donegal beaches. At Downings terraces of fill now completely conceal the frontal dunes, and extend seawards over parts of the back beach. The terraces were constructed to permit the seaward expansion of caravan parks. At Magheraroarty builders' rubble is habitually dumped on the narrow eroding neck of the Dooey sandspit. This practice may have started as a well-meaning attempt to stop erosion, but has long since become just a convenient method of waste disposal. At Rossnowlagh the owner of a block of dunes used terrestrial fill to build up an eroding dune scarp. The local authority was unhappy about this, but could take no action as it appeared that the landowner had acted within the law. At Narin terrestrial fill was used to back fill a trench as part of an otherwise environmentally sensitive scheme to tackle coastal erosion. The use of fill resulted in the growth of terrestrial weed vegetation on the embryo dunes. At Culdaff glacial till excavated during the construction of a new football pitch was disposed off by spreading it over the adjacent dunes. This had the unfortunate consequence of sealing the surface by creating an impermeable layer. Later the surface had to be rotavated to break the clay layer up.

persuaded to use the site provided and stop fly-tipping. Signs and prohibition notices at the site are also necessary. If entrances and gaps in the dunes are being used to provide access these should be closed with fences or bollards.

As with sand mining public education is the key to dealing with dumping. A concerned, vigilant public that will not accept the use of the beach and dunes as a rubbish tip is the best bulwark against this practice. However there are legal difficulties where the backshore lands are privately owned. In Ireland, for example, a landowner has a legal right to defend his property at its seaward limit *viz.* the Mean High Water mark. The relevant legislation does not specify what material can be used to do this, so it is unclear whether there is any prohibition on using terrestrial fill or rubble.

Issue: Harbours and piers

Photo 31. The pier at Downings, Co. Donegal adjoins the Blue Flag beach. Fishermen complain that the wakes from jetskis and powerboats make landings difficult.

Description: Many beaches lie adjacent to piers or small harbours (see photo 31). These may be used solely for recreation, or may have a mix of commercial and recreational uses. Examples of the former are commercial fishing, the servicing of aquaculture enterprises and small-scale ferry operations. There will occasionally be competition leading to conflict between the two broad groups of commercial and recreational users, a situation often exacerbated by the inexperience of the latter group. Examples of conflict include: competition for berthing space at the pier, danger of collisions due to congestion and irresponsible navigation, safety problems as children swim in the pier area and dive from its edge, pollution from fuel oil and fish debris, disruption to commercial operations due to the wakes from fast jet-skis and powerboats, and visitors' cars blocking commercial access to the pier (see case study 12). Quite apart from the inter-sectoral conflicts there can also be conflict within the sectors, e.g. between powerboats and sailing boats.

Case Study 12

At Downings in north Donegal the sheltered bay is ideal for water skiing, windsurfing and jet-skis, while the Blue Flag beach is a major attraction. There are, however, some user conflicts. Fishermen using the somewhat exposed pier adjacent to the beach complain that the wakes from powerboats and jet-skis are making it difficult for them to unload their catches. During the summer holiday season a jet-ski hire business operates from the pier and attracts large numbers of young people and children into the water. Water speed limits, zoning and the compulsory use of buoyed channels have been introduced recently to deal with these problems (see figure 4).

Response:

These conflicts between commercial and recreational interests can be difficult to resolve. There is a widespread perception, perhaps justified, that people making their living should have preferential use of an essential facility such as a pier or harbour. If a fundamental clash of interests occurs it would seem just that commercial users should prevail. However, ownership of the pier may complicate matters, particularly where it is built or maintained at public expense and even more so when it is explicitly intended to service watersports. In practice few fishermen demand sole rights to use pier or harbour facilities and sensitive zoning can remove many conflicts.

All craft should have to obey speed limits and where necessary keep to buoyed channels. Some activities should be banned where there are totally incompatible with commercial use of a pier. This certainly applies to swimming and sub-aqua diving on both safety and health grounds. In some cases it may also apply to jet-skis. This can present a problem in that they may have no alternative launch site. There are many reasons why it is desirable that the public should have access to piers and harbours including the fact that such places contribute greatly to the ambience of many seaside resorts. Certainly safety should be an important aspect of pier management, and water safety regulations, notices and equipment should be a part of the pier infrastructure. Nevertheless it would be a retrograde step if safety concerns led to the exclusion of the public.

Issue: Marina development and operation

Description: Although they are essentially recreational facilities marinas are dealt with in this section because they have a similar relationship to recreational beaches as the harbours and piers discussed above. Marina development is very much a growth area, and many existing and planned marinas lie close to sand beaches. Dredging of the marina basin and the approach channels can lead to some of the problems described in chapter 1 and sections 4.1 and 4.4 of chapter 4. There can be other environmental downsides, e.g. some marinas are built at the expense of beach, dune, mudflat and salt marsh habitats (see photo 32 and case study 13). They bring increased road traffic leading to congestion and road safety problems. Marina developments also bring pollution risks associated with waste disposal and oil spills. Unlike most piers and traditional harbours, where free access to the public is usually permitted, marinas often erect barriers and allow access only to boat owners. This applies both to private enterprises and those owned by local authorities. This brings the danger that marina development might compromise public access to the shore.

Photo 32. Marina construction at Lisfannon, Co. Donegal. This development has led to the destruction of salt marsh and dune habitat. Large volumes of dune sand have been removed from the site.

Response:

It is strongly suggested that marinas should be encouraged to apply for a Blue Flag award under the Foundation for Environmental Education in Europe (FEEE) scheme (see section 4.5). In this way they can be subject to similar safety, water quality and facilities standards as apply to Blue Flag beaches. In the case of new marinas, planning authorities should insist on detailed and rigorous environmental impact statements including mandatory physical/simulated wave and tidal current modelling of waste streams. Planners should also consider the implications of the development for the management of nearby recreational beaches. Offshore control systems such as water zoning, speed limits and buoyed navigation channels, and terrestrial control systems such as traffic and parking should be integrated with those of the beaches. Marina management plans should include adequate waste disposal mechanisms plus emergency plans to deal with oil spills and other accidents. Marinas also need their own safety infrastructure, e.g. lifebelts. It is important that authorities do not permit marina development or operation to interfere with public rights of way to the shore.

Case Study 13

In the late 1990s at Lisfannon, Co. Donegal, a leisure company began to develop a new marina on an area of foreshore for which it had earlier been granted a foreshore lease by the Department of the Marine and Natural Resources (DoMNR). The developers had no current planning permission from the local authority for the infrastructural elements located above MHW, e.g. service buildings and parking areas. The local authority became concerned when the marina company began to remove large quantities of beach and dune sand from the site. However, it was advised against taking legal action against the developer on the grounds that it could not be confident of proving jurisdiction in court (see case study 17 in section 4.5). The local authority's only option was to request the DoMNR to take action. After considerable inter-departmental delay, during which time the marina embankments were virtually completed, DoMNR issued a formal warning to the developer and work stopped.

Issue: Fishing

Description: Apart from the potential pier-based conflicts described above, commercial sea fishing is not usually a beach management issue because it takes place well offshore. In contrast some types of inshore fishing can occasionally lead to conflict with recreational activities. Shore-attached stake and bag nets are sometimes positioned around rocky promontories close to sand beaches, while the same areas are often used for lobster and crab pots. The presence of these activities close to shore can lead to disputes between the fishermen and the owners of powered craft and windsurfers who risk snagging on the fishing gear. Beach casting is recreational rather than commercial and tends to take place when there are few people on the beach: nevertheless here too there is potential for friction as fishermen and other beach users interfere with each other's freedom of movement.

Response:

Inshore fishing can be a sensitive issue because these traditional fishing practices have often been carried on by the same families in the same places for generations. Careful zoning of recreational watersports to avoid fishing areas is the obvious method of reducing these conflicts although, as is so often the case, jet-skis in particular may have nowhere to go if the rocky shoreline also is out of bounds. Codes of conduct for watersports should emphasise the need to give a wide berth to areas where fishing buoys or anchor ropes are visible in the water.

Issue: Aquaculture

Description: There has been a huge expansion of aquaculture in recent years, e.g. in the estuaries of northwest and southwest Ireland. Farms usually concentrate on either finfish or shellfish such as mussels and oysters. Objections have been raised to the visual intrusion that the farms cause in scenic areas. There are also concerns that the waste generated contributes to the increased frequency of algal blooms and generation of the toxins responsible for shellfish contamination (see case study 2 in section 4.1). As with commercial fishermen, aquaculture operators who use a general access pier or harbour may be involved in conflicts with recreational users as described above. User conflicts can also arise offshore. Cages are usually set too far offshore to present any problems for swimmers, but conflicts can arise with water sports carried out away from the beach such as sailing, powerboating, water-skiing and jet-skiing. The presence of the farms interferes with their preferred runs, and since the farms are often not mapped they can be a navigation hazard. For their part the aquaculture interests are annoyed by damage to their gear.

Response:

The need to maximise employment opportunities in rural areas has often ensured that authorities tend to look favourably on applications for aquaculture licences. In some instances where recreational interests have been damaged this policy may be short-sighted, because in the long run the economic value of recreation may be higher than that of aquaculture, even if more difficult to quantify. Potential conflicts with recreational water users should be considered as one of the factors at the planning stage of aquaculture and locational decisions altered where necessary. One fundamental problem in achieving an integrated approach is that in some jurisdictions the body which controls terrestrial planning, including recreational infrastructure, has no control over development either in the inter-tidal area or offshore. (This is discussed in more detail in section 4.5.) Once fish farms are in place recreational water users should ideally be zoned away, but this is not always possible, given restrictions on space. Codes of Conduct should advise water users to stay well clear of the cages.

Issue: Collection of shellfish and bait from the foreshore

Description: Among the traditional practices which survive to the present day on the foreshore is that of gathering shellfish or bait from inter-tidal rocks, beaches and, more commonly, tidal flats. The latter are unlikely to be used for recreation because of their relatively high mud content, so no beach management problems should arise. On sand beaches the practice typically operates in a low intensity manner and generally only manual methods are used.

Response:

This activity is rarely a problem on recreational sand beaches, and can be considered a sustainable traditional practice. Beach managers should look closely at any tendency to replace traditional manual methods with mechanical rakes and harvesters that might adversely affect beach fauna. If there are any concerns either about location or methods it is best to use negotiation and compromise. Given the sensitivity of interfering with traditional practices, it is generally unwise to have recourse to formal legal enforcement if only because the courts might well find in favour of these "prescriptive" rights.

Issue: Development in sand dunes

Description: The appeal of the coast as a place to live and for recreation has made it economically attractive for owners of coastal dunes to sell sites for development (or to develop the dunes themselves). This trend is most obvious where the dunes are divided among a number of private owners. Publicly owned dunes are less likely to be developed because authorities come under public pressure to manage their dunes according to a conservation or amenity model. Indeed the dunes may have come into public ownership in order to ensure their preservation.

The development process is often aided by favourable attitudes from planning authorities who wish to maximise economic development in relatively remote coastal areas with few other resources. The word "development" carries connotations of progress and enlightenment which are often inappropriate descriptions of the destruction of habitat and environmental degradation which local planning authorities have allowed to take place in once attractive and extensive dune systems. Paradoxically the designation of the more outstanding dune systems as protected areas may have been a factor in the accelerated degradation of non-designated systems. This occurred because authorities and individuals took non-designation as a signal for development (see section 4.5).

Photo 33. Haphazard distribution of fixed caravans on a site in the dunes at Tramore, near Rosbeg, Co. Donegal. The brick building on the left is the site service block.

Amongst the most common forms of development are roads, playing fields, golf courses, play areas, caravan and mobile home parks (see photo 33), car parks, toilet blocks, holiday homes, and a plethora of commercial buildings servicing the visitor market e.g. hotels, cafes and shops. The footprint of impact associated with

such developments often extends well away from the structures themselves. Some of these impacts are included in the plans, e.g. levelling or moulding of dune topography, septic tanks, trenches for services such as water mains, access roads and turning areas. Other impacts are incidental but predictable, e.g. trampling damage to dunes associated with pedestrian concentrations around public use developments. In many areas development of dunes has been on such a scale that it has resulted in the fragmentation and in some cases the virtual destruction of the former dune system (see case study 14). From an ecological viewpoint the dune field may become so fragmented that the surviving pieces become "grass islands" which cannot function effectively as habitat because of their isolation. A further downside is that development may later lead to a demand for shoreline armour because valuable property is threatened by natural shoreline erosion (see case study 15).

Response:

On some dune systems, particularly where erosion is very rapid, development should not be permitted at all. This should also be the case where the dunes have a high habitat or amenity value (even if not designated). The management aim should be to conserve and enhance such sites.

On sites where development is allowed it should not be permitted in the frontal dunes nearest the beach. One way to implement this restriction is to establish a set-back line from Mean High Water (ECOPRO 1996). A set-back line defines the landward margin of a shore-contact zone within which there is virtually a blanket ban on development. Set-back zones should be an integral part of planning policy rather than *ad hoc* devices used to manage given sites. Some jurisdictions use an across-the-board figure, with set-back distances typically in the range 30-100m. Denmark has a general 100m setback from a beach, but this is increased to 3km for holiday homes and hotels. In Ireland, Co. Wexford has a general 50m set-back on soft coasts. This type of standard set-back is most suitable where erosion is cyclic; the set-back ensures that no development can take place inside the erosion/accretion envelope.

Photo 34. Progressive shoreline erosion at Rossnowlagh, Co. Donegal. The WW2 blockhouse, originally built in the duneline in 1940, now lies on the beach 34m from the base of the retreating dune scarp.

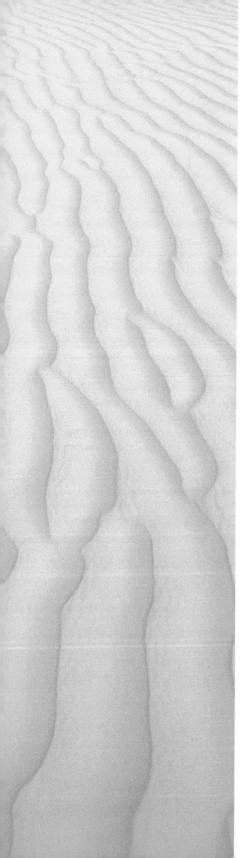

However, where erosion is progressive MHW is retreating steadily landwards, and over time any designated set-back zone decreases in width. It is very difficult to shift a set-back zone landward if development has taken place behind it, so to avoid controversial litigation and high compensation payments it is best to establish wide set-back zones in the first instance. In such cases the dimensions of the zone should be related to objective site-specific parameters. One approach to this is to calculate set-back distance using a formula: *set-back distance = mean annual erosion rate x factor*. In South Carolina USA a factor of 40 is used, with distances measured from the most seaward dune. Calculation of a site-specific set-back requires data on the erosion, flooding and accretion history of the site. This can be obtained from a combination of repeated surveys, and anecdotal and documentary evidence including comparative analysis of maps and aerial photographs. Landward of the set-back zone, where development is allowed, there can still be a need for restrictions. In addition to its general set-back (usually 30m) the state of Maine in the USA uses flood maps combined with federal flood insurance strategy to control development. No development will be permitted in areas that have ever experienced prior flood damage. In areas where the surface elevation lies below that of the highest flood in 100 years houses must be built on posts so that their floor levels will be a minimum of 0.3m above the flood level. From time to time as the shoreline shifts the flood maps are redrawn (Kelley *et al.* 1989).

In dune areas without formal set-back restrictions planners should try to maintain the open, natural quality of the landscape. Consequently they should favour proposals that require few, if any, permanent structures. Building development should be directed towards less fragile areas underlain by bedrock or till, but not at the expense of environmental quality. Visual intrusion should be avoided, e.g. houses on headlands, and high standards of design and construction should be demanded. In practice there should be a general presumption against proposals that demand substantial earth moving, or which involve laying down hard surfaces such as tarmac, concrete or quarry-stone hard core. In this regard it is vitally important that the cumulative effects of existing individual developments and new proposals should be kept in mind. In the past golf courses or playing fields have been regarded as suitable forms of development in duneland; however these often involve a surprising degree of earth moving and when in use demand an artificial sward. Developers should also be obliged to accommodate the predictable footprint effects of their proposals and take steps to deal with them at the planning stage, e.g. the provision of fenced boardwalk paths to channel pedestrians between a caravan park and the beach. As a matter of policy the planning authority should make it clear that it will not grant requests for armouring to protect existing or new dune development.

4.5: Issues primarily related to jurisdiction, tenure, administration and regulation

Issue: Jurisdiction

Description: Legal jurisdiction over beaches and dunes is fundamental to their management. Given the huge variation among countries, the complexity of the legislation and the many anomalies these notes can only make a few general points. The case studies illustrate some of the issues with examples from Ireland. See Gibson (1999) for discussion of these issues in a European and international context, and Crosbie (1995) for the situation in Ireland.

In many countries there is a terrestrial/marine jurisdictional divide which can have adverse consequences for beach and dune management. If the administrative boundary is at high water the beach and dunes, which are physically intimately related, are under the jurisdiction of different government departments. In some cases management aims and outcomes can be diametrically opposed, e.g. it is theoretically possible that a terrestrial planning authority might follow a conservation model on supra-tidal dunes while simultaneously a marine authority promotes industrial development on the adjacent foreshore. While there may be few cases as extreme as this many problems and inefficiencies arise when the terrestrial and marine authorities have different philosophies and working methods, and where communication between them is poorly developed (see case studies 13 and 16). Terrestrial planning authorities tend to be much more proactive and have a higher profile than marine authorities which tend to act as relatively

Case Study 16

In Ireland terrestrial planning powers are exercised by local authorities (County Councils) which act under the aegis of the Department of the Environment and Local Government. The administrative area of a local authority normally extends only to Mean High Water (MHW). Therefore the planning powers of the Council also extend to this limit. The only legislative control available for inter-tidal and sub-tidal areas lies in the Foreshore Acts administered by the Department of the Marine and Natural Resources (DoMNR). However, the Foreshore Acts were not designed as planning instruments and they lack the consultation, public transparency and accountability aspects which are typical of sophisticated planning instruments. Linkages between the terrestrial and marine sectors are weak and there is considerable legal confusion over the relationship between terrestrial planning permissions and foreshore licences and leases. In 1999 the Minister for the Marine made an attempt to harmonise the activities of his Department with those of the planning authorities. He stated that future foreshore licences and leases would only be granted to developers who obtain planning permission from the appropriate local authority for the entire development including areas below MHW.

Photo 35. The beach, dune and saltmarsh complex at Lisfannon, Co. Donegal is legally regarded as part of the inter-tidal zone because the most recent large-scale OS map shows MHW lying at the base of the embankment on the centre-left.

passive holding companies for the State's inter-tidal and sub-tidal property. Split jurisdiction can also lead to competition between departments, and a culture of secretiveness can develop which makes rational and integrated approaches to coastal problems very difficult. Further problems arise when the jurisdictional boundaries are based on obsolete maps that bear little relation to the current topography (see photo 35 and case study 17).

Case Study 17

In Ireland the problem of split jurisdiction between terrestrial and marine authorities is sometimes compounded by the fact that the legal basis for the position of Mean High Water (MHW), and therefore the boundary between terrestrial and marine administrative areas, is the most recent large scale map produced by the national mapping agency. At Lisfannon, Co. Donegal, the relevant map, published in 1905, is based on a field survey carried out in 1903. Since then an extensive beach, sand dune and salt marsh complex has developed up to 250m seaward of the 1903 MHW. However, legal jurisdiction is based on the now obsolete map, so the entire area is regarded as inter-tidal foreshore and as such falls within the administrative area of the Department of the Marine and Natural Resources (DoMNR) rather than that of the local authority Donegal County Council. In consequence the Planning Acts administered by the Council do not apply in this area and control is through the Foreshore Acts.

Response:

Beach and dune management is undoubtedly made more difficult by split or anomalous jurisdiction, but the beach manager will usually have to work within these constraints, since it is very unlikely that anything can be done at the local level to modify such a complex legal concept as jurisdiction. Ideally the objectives of integrated coastal zone management can best be achieved by one unitary authority spanning the terrestrial-marine divide. Where this is not the case it can be created by extending terrestrial planning control out to at least low water level and ideally out to the territorial limit. This will allow harmonisation of both terrestrial and marine activities, prevent inconsistencies and close off loopholes in legislation. Both of the strategies above face problems from the inertia of Government structures, inter-departmental conflicts and rivalries, and the tendency of departments to resist any attempts to reduce their areas of control. A less drastic method of achieving harmonisation is to set up joint ICZM committees at government level with input and representation from all departments with coastal responsibilities. Less formally integration can be promoted in a voluntary coastal forum or partnership to which the existing authorities send representatives and where they commit themselves to integrated approaches to the management of both terrestrial and marine elements. Examples of coastal fora are the Bantry Bay Forum in Ireland, the Forth Estuary Forum in Scotland and the Dorset Coast Forum in England.

Obviously the problems created by obsolete maps can be resolved by regular updating, but there are financial and practical limits to the survey frequency of published maps. In any case, on a sandy coast a map only a few years old can be rendered obsolete by rapid shoreline retreat. Planning regulations could be modified to allow the use of non-published survey data and maps produced by new digital technologies where these are more up to date than published paper maps. Using GPS and GIS techniques it is now possible to produce very quickly and relatively cheaply a highly accurate map of a specific section of coast including the present tidal limits. This work could be done by the planning authority or national mapping agency with costs passed on to the developer where appropriate.

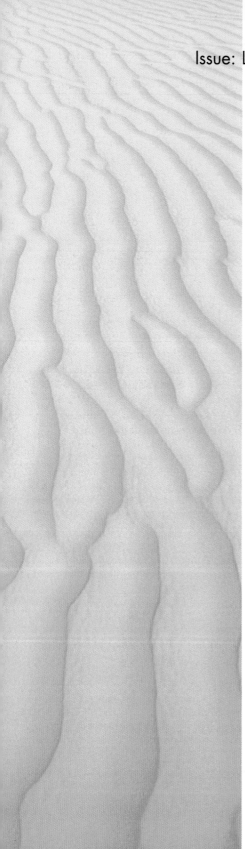

Issue: Land tenure

Description: Land tenure type is an important constraint on beach and dune management. There are a variety of tenure types, e.g. private ownership, corporate private ownership, tenancy, common ownership, joint ownership and public ownership. The access aspects of land tenure are discussed in section 4.2.

Private ownership of dune areas, with the land fenced off into separate holdings, is common in Ireland and Britain. Some beaches are also privately owned but more usually they are held in State tenure. In general, private tenure by a number of owners is the worst-case scenario for management. The site cannot be managed as a coherent unit as each owner pursues a personal agenda that is unlikely to consider the health of the system as a whole. Ownership of an entire dune system by a single individual is usually preferable as the site can at least be managed as a unit, even if not always in an environmentally enlightened manner. It may still, however, be threatened by piecemeal development of individual plots. One practical benefit is that managers and responsible authorities do not have to negotiate with multiple owners.

Examples of corporate private owners include conservation-orientated NGOs (e.g. the RSPB and The National Trust in the UK), sports associations especially golf clubs, and port and harbour authorities. Some of these bodies are hybrid in that they have input from publicly elected representatives. In the case of port authorities the enabling legislation also conveys jurisdiction in that they have the power to make bye-laws. However, they are still generally subject to the overriding jurisdiction of government departments.

Golf clubs are among the most ubiquitous of corporate private owners. Opinion is divided on the environmental impacts of golf courses. Some courses make minimum changes to the natural morphology of the site while others engineer designed morphological elements. In many cases golf courses have a lower conservation value than sensitively grazed privately owned dunes. The course is an artificial sward due to mowing and the use of fertiliser and pesticides, with the only real conservation value lying in islands among the mown areas. Golf courses are also more likely than private landowners to erect rock armour defences, e.g. at Portrush, Co. Antrim and Portsalon, Co. Donegal. The more positive side of golf club tenure is that the existence of a course may protect dunes from building development. From this perspective a golf course does at least function as an open area of amenity grassland which is preferable to the proliferation of holiday home development which might have occurred otherwise. In addition the corporate ownership structure means that no one member can decide to sell the land to cash in on a development boom; in any case it is unlikely (although not unknown) that a golf club would consider selling its course.

As would be expected private conservation bodies set the highest value on environmental considerations (see photo 37), although occasionally their specific activities might be questioned, e.g. the practice of beach parking on some National Trust properties in the UK. Port and harbour authorities are unlikely to exercise direct control over a recreational beach, especially in a rural area. Nevertheless many smaller harbours lie adjacent to sand beaches and their activities will affect the beach and/or its users. Some of these small ports are dominantly or solely used for recreational boating but other have a mixture of recreational and commercial uses. Port authorities do have obligations to consider environmental and conservation objectives, but their primary interest will always lie in economic development. Traditionally they have a very large degree of autonomy in their operations, sometimes prompting accusations that they are laws unto themselves. Statutory planning bodies tend to give a sympathetic hearing to port authority proposals for landfill, dredging and armour emplacement on the grounds that these are necessary if the port is to remain economically viable.

In Ireland renting of sand dunes for agricultural purposes is not common because of the relatively low productivity of the land. Where dunes are rented they are normally used for grazing, e.g. at Ballyteigue, Co. Wexford and Rossbeigh, Co. Kerry. It is more common to find sand dunes rented for non-agricultural purposes such as sport (see photos 36 and 43), or tourism–related commerce. Land rented for agriculture is unlikely to suffer building development, but sports clubs and commercial enterprises on long term leases may construct a variety of buildings and facilities such as roads, car parks, club houses, pavilions, shops etc.

Photo 36. The Narin-Portnoo golf course in Co. Donegal dates from 1931 and is located on dunes rented from local farmers. In Ireland a sports club that has leased land for a period of at least 21 years (a 'sporting lease') has legal protection against eviction.

Photo 37. The Blue Flag and UK Seaside Award beach of Portstewart Strand in Co. Derry, with the River Bann in the foreground. The National Trust owns the major part of the dunes, but leases the inter-tidal beach from the Crown Estate.

Common ownership can exist in the sense of a public common open to all, or in the sense of joint ownership by specified individuals. Common tenure can be a positive benefit to sustainable beach and dune management. Dunes held in either form of common tenure are usually free of building development or potentially damaging coastal defences because landowners will not invest money developing or defending land that is not their personal property. In the absence of building development the generally low value of the land inhibits the construction of expensive defences. However, common or joint ownership can have its own specific management problems. An example is the risk of severe overgrazing of dune grassland (see case study 18), while other problems result from the very fact that commonage is, or is perceived to be, public property. Since no one individual owns the land the access must be permanently open. The unfortunate consequence of this is that public access remains uncontrolled leading to dune degradation and littering as the public avail of property that is access and rent-free. Where the dunes are in joint ownership such visitors are technically trespassing, but they are unlikely to be challenged (see case study 19). In Ireland the uncontrolled use of ATVs and scrambling motorcycles, and the dumping of old cars, are common consequences of free access to coastal lands held in common. Sometimes privately owned coastal lands are perceived as a common. This occurs if no obvious control or management takes

Some countries have national beach awards. Among the best known is the Seaside Award in the UK. This was introduced in 1992 and is also administered by the Tidy Britain Group. The Seaside Award is an annual award given to beaches that comply with the mandatory standard of the European Bathing Water Directive and are clean, safe, well managed and provide current and previous water quality information. The beach need not necessarily be one of those 'identified' under the directive. Unlike the Blue Flag scheme the Seaside Award distinguishes between resort beaches which must fulfil 28 land-based criteria, and rural beaches with more limited facilities which must meet 12 criteria. The latter are expected to be clean, relatively safe for swimming, provide life-saving equipment and regularly monitored. The Tidy Britain Group is currently piloting a Green Coast award in Wales. This is an award specifically targeted at relatively remote, unspoilt rural beaches with guideline standard water quality and which have sound environmental management.

In 2000 there were 70 Blue Flag beaches in the Republic of Ireland, while the UK had 57 of which 8 were in Northern Ireland. In the same year the Tidy Britain Group designated 272 Seaside Award beaches in the UK, of which 8, all resorts, were in Northern Ireland. 154 (57%) of the awards were rural. Some beaches, e.g. all those designated in Northern Ireland, won both the Blue Flag and Seaside Awards (see photo 39). In 2000 eighty local authorities and private beach operators in the UK were participating in either or both of the Tidy Britain Group schemes. Both the Blue Flag and Seaside Awards have published a set of national beach standards. Details can be found at **http://www.blueflag.org** and **http://www.feee.org** for the Blue Flag scheme, and **http://www.tidybritain.org.uk** for the Seaside Award.

Although not strictly designations there are other awards and recommendations which have acquired considerable status, and are greatly coveted by those responsible for managing beaches. A good example in the UK is inclusion in the *Good Beach Guide* published annually every spring since 1988 by the Marine Conservation Society, an environmental charity focussing on marine pollution issues. The beaches recommended have achieved the highest water quality standards and are not affected by inadequately treated sewage. In the 2000 guide 215 beaches are recommended covering all regions of the UK. Information can be found at **http://www.goodbeachguide.co.uk**.

Response:

Recreational designations and recommendations are generally welcome since they focus attention and bring resources to bear on desirable goals such as water quality improvement, cleanliness and environmental education. Beach managers usually find it much easier to argue a case for funding and other resources when the aim is to achieve or maintain an award.

However, there is a real risk that competition between local authorities on a "Blue Flag league table" may lead to inappropriate designations. In some cases the concentration of resources on award beaches leads to the neglect of other attractive sites. The ideal might be to have a continuum of recreational designations ranging from intensively managed Blue Flag beaches with a lot of infrastructure at one end of the scale, to natural unspoilt sites with sensitive low profile management at the other. This would help to alleviate the "Blue Flag or nothing" syndrome found in Ireland. For various reasons, among which are environmental and cost-effectiveness concerns, it may be advisable not to pursue Blue Flag awards for the majority of rural beaches. In particular authorities should consider carefully before seeking this high status recreational designation for pristine sites of great ecological and habitat merit. Even with superior management such sites may be degraded by the increased visitor numbers generated by the award. They might be better served by either an explicit conservation model, or an approach which is a careful blend of recreational and conservation objectives. The Blue Flag model works best for urban beaches and those with historically high visitor numbers. It suffers from the weakness that it tends to be administered as an inflexible template with limited potential to adjust to local conditions. The criteria for rural beaches in the UK Seaside Award and the pilot Green Coast Award in Wales are generally more suitable than those of the Blue Flag for rural beaches. These two award schemes are specific to the UK, but beach managers elsewhere in Europe could usefully follow their standards, which offer a pragmatic model for the management of rural beaches.

In some cases a specific requirement of designation may conflict with other values, especially environmental values. One example of this is the Blue Flag and UK Seaside Award criterion that seaweed must be removed from the beach. While it is true that the smell of seaweed and the insects it attracts are unattractive to tourists, the weed is part of the natural beach cycle and should not be classed as litter (see sections 4.3 and 4.4). However, as long as the bodies responsible for designation maintain this criterion, beach managers must comply if they want the awards. The pilot Green Coast award in Wales does not require the removal of seaweed.

Issue: Conservation designations

Description: Conservation designations exist at the local, national, European and global levels. They are independent of jurisdictional and tenure boundaries. Indeed SACs and SPAs are theoretically transnational. Given the huge variety of designations, especially at the national level, the summary below will take the situation in Ireland as an example. Gibson (1999) discusses environmental designations as part of a general overview of coastal zone laws in and outside of Europe.

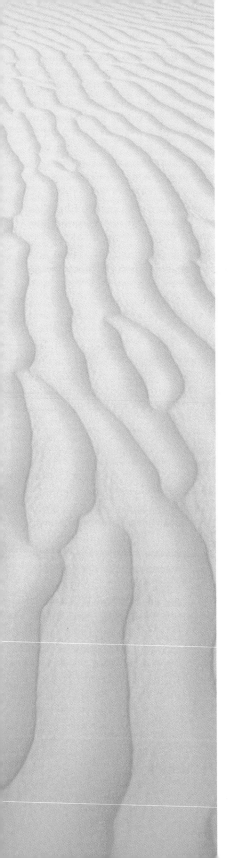

Hickie (1996) has summarised the various environmental designations that apply in Ireland. The main national, European and global designations are administered by Dúchas, the national statutory conservation body. In all there are eighteen nature and amenity designations, not all of which are relevant to the beach/dune environment. Many sites have overlapping multiple designations, for example North Bull Island, Co. Dublin has nine.

The primary national nature conservation designation is that of Natural Heritage Area (NHA) which covers 7% of the national territory. However, currently NHA is a proposed designation to replace an earlier one, Area of Scientific Interest (ASI), and has no legal basis until an amendment is passed to the legislation. All other national (e.g. Statutory Nature Reserve, National Park), European (e.g. SPA, SAC) and global (e.g. Ramsar Site) nature designations overlap with and are subsets of the basic NHA designation. Of the seven Donegal LIFE sites six lie wholly or partly within proposed NHAs, while the remaining site borders an NHA. NHAs are protected via controls on planning permission, e.g. applications must be referred to the statutory conservation body, and state and EU funding will be denied to projects which might damage habitats.

Apart from nature conservation designations environmental objectives are pursued by local authorities through amenity or landscape designations that serve to control human use and development. Many of these apply to coastal areas. These designations (e.g. Areas of Special Control, Special Amenity Area Order) form part of the local authorities' development plans. In the County Donegal Development Plan (2000) landscapes are classified into 3 broad categories with Category 3 describing scenic largely intact natural landscapes containing few, if any, man-made structures. Development controls are very strict in Category 3; for example it is County Council policy to refuse planning applications for new houses within this category. Many beach and dune systems, including three of the LIFE sites, lie in areas with Category 3 status. Three other LIFE sites are classified as Category 2, with the remaining site in a Category 1 zone.

The Department of Agriculture Food and Forestry administers a national (but EC-required and partially funded) agri-environmental initiative known as the Rural Environment Protection Scheme (REPS) which is designed to achieve conservation objectives by offering farmers compensation to modify or maintain their farming practices. The whole country is eligible, but higher rates (20%) are payable within NHAs. Farmers at the Donegal LIFE sites of Portsalon, Magheraroarty and Narin take part in the REPS scheme.

The main European conservation designations with relevance to beaches and dunes are that of Special Protection Area (SPA) under the Birds Directive (79/409/EEC) and Special Area of Conservation (SAC) under the later Habitats Directive (92/43/EEC). As is the case

with NHAs, the SACs still only have candidate status and will not be formally designated until legislation is amended. However, the sites are already protected because the EC Regulations state that candidate sites are to be regarded in law as if they are already designated. This is an important factor in the conservation of these sites as the designation process in Ireland is several years behind schedule. SPAs and SACs are designated because of the presence of endangered species or habitats, not to conserve visual amenity or access. Within the designated areas there are strict controls on development with strong legal backing. In addition authorities can control activities outside the designated areas which might have impacts inside them. Of the seven LIFE sites in Donegal two are wholly included and three are partly included within a cSAC. In the partial cases all of the inter-tidal beach lies within the designated area. The remaining two sites each border an SPA. The beaches at North Bull Island Co. Dublin are within an SPA.

At the global level designations which can potentially include beaches and dunes are Ramsar Wetland Site and World Heritage Site. There are 21 Ramsar sites in Ireland, all but two of which are State owned. Several of these include beach and dune systems, e.g. North Bull Island Co. Dublin and Raven Point Co. Wexford. Of the three World Heritage Sites in Ireland one, the Giant's Causeway in Co. Antrim, was nominated for its natural coastal features but the site consists of a rocky coastal stretch without sand beaches. The coastal landscape was a factor in the nomination of only one of the twelve sites currently designated in Britain, and that lies on the now uninhabited island of St. Kilda. However, it is the stated intention of the British government to nominate the Dorset and East Devon Coast in southern England. If this succeeds many recreational beach and dune systems will be included in the designated area. Information on World Heritage Sites can be obtained at **http://www.unesco.org/whc**.

Response:

Beach managers should know which, if any, conservation designations apply to their sites and the legal implications. Conservation designation is generally welcome as it can bring status and protection, and can help in the release of management funds and other resources. There also may be opportunities for the development of eco-tourism and educational activities. In Ireland there is a huge variation across the various designations in their legal backing and the powers available. This leads to a great disparity in the degree of protection offered, ranging from virtually none in some of the national designations to strong statutory protection for the European designations of SPA and SAC. Designation alone does not protect; the statutory authorities must have the manpower and funding necessary to implement the positive management the designated sites need. Surprisingly, the prestigious international designations of Ramsar Site and World Heritage Site bestow no protection *per se*; one reason why sites are designated is that they are already protected by other designations, e.g. Statutory Nature Reserve or SPA in the Ramsar case. One of the advantages of multiple designation is that a site can take advantage of the strongest protection available in the set.

There can be a degree of incompatibility between environmental designation and recreational use, and in some cases designation for environmental objectives can lead to considerable restrictions on the use and development of a beach. High intensity recreational or amenity use is generally incompatible with conservation aims. The major mismatch concerns the recreational need for vehicle access and parking close to the beach, which contrasts with the general conservation aim to avoid construction on site (see case study 20). Trampling by pedestrians and the litter generated by recreational visitors are other common problems.

The ideal situation is to manage a fairly large coastal stretch for multiple uses in a balanced integrated manner. With careful planning recreational visitor numbers can be concentrated on those areas that can take the pressure, while simultaneously visitor numbers are strictly controlled in areas of designated high quality habitat where geomorphological processes and/or ecological successions must be allowed to operate without interruption. This type of management can be accomplished without heavy-handed regimentation of the public. Most objectives can be achieved by careful siting and layout of roads, car parks, paths and visitor facilities. A fine example of this management approach can be seen on the Sefton coast in eastern England (Atkinson and Houston, 1993).

The beach manager is likely to be centrally involved in decisions regarding recreational designations, but specialist scientists and wardens from statutory government bodies will play the dominant role in conservation designations. Occasionally there may be friction between personnel in these groups, with the recreational interest sometimes irked by the restrictions put on their activities by cautious conservation bodies. However, it is in the best interests of all for the beach manager to maintain close and cordial relationships with the local representatives of national bodies. In many places recreation seems to coexist quite happily with environmental designation, e.g. several cSACs in Co. Donegal contain Blue Flag beaches.

Problems can also arise where there is a lack of integration of the objectives of environmental designation with general economic objectives (see case study 21). It should also be noted that designation does not guarantee public access, e.g. in Northern Ireland part of the restricted military base in the sand dunes at Magilligan, Co. Derry is designated as an Area of Special Scientific Interest (ASSI). This UK national designation is concerned only with the preservation of the site's inherent "scientific" value, not its public amenity interest.

Photo 40. Development in sand dunes at Rossnowlagh, Co. Donegal.

As with recreational designations one of the downsides is that non-designated sites may suffer from neglect, as all resources are concentrated on a few prize sites. Non-designated sites may suffer from over-development because of a general view that such sites must have little conservation value and therefore are suitable for large-scale development. This perception can become something of a self-fulfilling prophecy. At Rossnowlagh, Co. Donegal it can be asked which came first - the degradation of the dunes which meant that the site was not considered worthy of designation, or the failure to designate at an early stage which led almost inevitably to degradation (see photo 40, and case study 14 in section 4.4).

Issue: Legal regulation of activities

Description: There are a number of reasons why certain activities may need to be regulated on occasion. It may be because they pose a hazard to health and safety (e.g. cars being driven recklessly), degrade the site (e.g. littering or dune erosion), cause annoyance or generally lessen the enjoyment of beach users (e.g. noise pollution or anti-social behaviour). Voluntary measures such as codes of conduct are useful and are often all that are needed to curb unwanted activities. However their success is dependent on the co-operation of beach users, which is not always forthcoming. Technical solutions can be used to regulate activities, for instance bollards, buoys and fences are useful ways of controlling the movement of vehicles. Technical solutions have the disadvantages of being limited in scope and expensive. In some circumstances it may be necessary to use legal means to regulate activities.

Response:

In most countries there are laws to deal with specific activities such as dog control or littering. However, there is a lack of legislation that can: (a) deal with the wide range of activities that take place on rural beaches; (b) manage the beach as a whole, on both sides of MHW; and (c) manage beach use effectively over both the short and the long time scales. The use of bye-laws on beaches provide an opportunity for local authorities to rectify these shortcomings.

At present in Ireland, bye-laws are used in a number of different ways (MacLeod et al. 2000). They are being used to prohibit certain acts on the beach and dunes such as: littering; driving cars; playing golf; riding horses; making excessive noise; gambling; disorderly behaviour; vandalism; games; trading; drinking; lighting fires; camping; obstruction. They are also being used to regulate certain activities and limit them to defined times and places. Regulated activities include: horse riding; jet-skiing; driving; dog walking; driving speed boats; water skiing; surfing and windsurfing. Experience in England suggests that, despite some shortcomings, bye-laws have a role to play in coastal management. A recent report

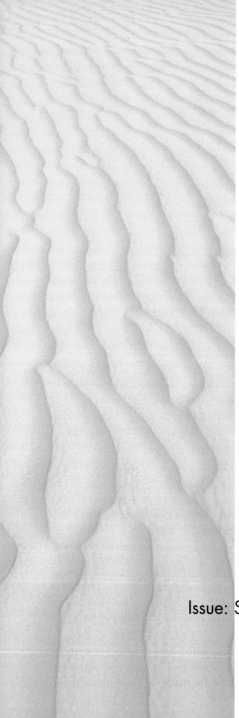

recommended the use of updated bye-law making powers for local authorities and suggested that local authorities "should be given more general bye-law powers to regulate activities affecting the wider environment" (DETR 1998, p3).

Transparency is vital and may be aided by having those affected participate in the development of the bye-laws. So far there have not been any major problems in achieving compliance with the bye-laws in Ireland; however most of them have only been in force for a short period of time. While any authorised person has the power to tell those in breach of a bye-law to stop an activity, to issue fines and to take names and addresses, in practice it could be impossible to deal with mass non-compliance. It is therefore more important to prevent non-compliance than to stop it. In order to achieve this, the bye-laws require the support of the local communities and of the majority of beach users. This support could be nurtured by adopting a bottom up approach to the development of the bye-laws, and by ensuring that the reasoning behind them was clearly explained to beach users. In addition, public participation in the formulation of beach bye-laws helps to identify the beach management issues that the public believe require action and encourages communication and learning amongst the participants.

It should be borne in mind that bye-laws may often be able only to control a problem rather than solve it, i.e. they may deal with the symptoms but not the underlying causes. As such there is a danger that they may simply hide or displace problems. For example, banning the use of dune buggies at one site may lead to them being used more at another site. In this instance it may be necessary to provide a dedicated area for dune buggies, and advice or training for their owners in addition to banning them from certain areas. In many instances bye-laws would be best employed as part of a wider long-term strategy that sought to find solutions to the underlying causes of beach management problems.

Issue: Signage

Description: Signage is an important aspect of beach management. It has a range of uses including providing warnings about hazards, highlighting facilities, outlining and explaining management initiatives, and requesting compliance. Most beach management involves some level of signage, so some thought should be given to how it can be most effectively utilised.

Response:

The exact purpose of the sign should be clarified at the outset. Careful consideration should be given to whether or not a sign is capable of achieving the task it is intended to. Signs are often

DONEGAL CO. COUNCIL
PLEASE KEEP THIS
BEACH SAFE FOR
ALL USERS.

PARKING TO LEFT OF
CONES ONLY.

NO DRIVING OTHER THAN
TO & FROM PARKING
AREA.

SPEED NOT TO
EXCEED 10mph

BREACHES OF THESE
CONDITIONS SHOULD BE
REPORTED & REGISTRATION
NUMBERS NOTED.

**NO
DUMPING
ON
BEACH**

Photo 41 The beach entrance at Downings Co. Donegal. Although a prime location, any further signage at this beach entrance would be counter-productive.

erected because they are an easy response, rather than an effective one. If it is decided that a sign is to be erected, then its location and design need to be chosen. A location should be chosen where the sign will be seen by those that it is intended for without detracting from existing signage. If too many signs are in close proximity then the result can be a confusing and ineffective array (see photo 41). It is therefore important that new signs are co-ordinated with existing ones. A location should also be chosen where the sign does not spoil the view or the scenic quality of the site. The design of the sign will depend on its purpose. Obviously a sign that is meant to warn a driver about an immediate hazard will be quite different from one that is meant to be read at leisure by someone in a picnic area. In all cases clarity of meaning is essential - jargon and ambiguities should be avoided. The mixture of words and images will vary from sign to sign; however all signs should be made, as far as possible, to withstand vandalism and the elements.

Issue: Cultural and socio-economic constraints on beach management

Description: Beach and dune management must take into account cultural and socio-economic factors that act as constraints on rational site management. These factors tend to be most powerful in rural areas and their power should not be underestimated.

Cultural constraints exist at several scales. In Ireland the most fundamental constraint lies in the nature of the public bodies which ultimately control the management and development of the coast. Typically these statutory authorities have weak often poorly defined powers, are under-funded, and have relatively few staff on the ground to implement their policies. This has led to the development of an informal, highly pragmatic, management culture whereby authorities try to persuade landowners, developers and the public to

Case Study 22

At Carrickfin in northwest Co. Donegal the sole runway of a regional airport lies close to a beautiful beach and sand dune system (see photo 5 in chapter 3). Built in 1976 the airfield is located in one of the few feasible sites available in this rugged terrain. In practice environmental values were sacrificed to accommodate a facility regarded as necessary for the region's economic development. The sacrifice of environmental values in favour of economic development continues. The beach and dunes were designated as a candidate Special Area of Conservation in 1997, and the site was awarded a Blue Flag in 1999. Despite these clear indications of the environmental and recreational quality of the site, the local planning authority in 1999 sanctioned the building of a new aeroplane spraying plant beside the terminal building. There were vociferous local objections on aesthetic and environmental grounds, but ultimately employment arguments held sway in this remote area which has seen little benefit from Ireland's economic resurgence in the 1990s. The local authority's decision to give planning permission was appealed to the national planning authority, but the decision was confirmed. However, in May 2000 campaigners were granted a full judicial review of the decision.

Case Study 23

At Carrickfin the beach and dunes are included within a cSAC. In 1998 Ireland's national conservation authority expressed concern that dune vegetation was being damaged by visitor cars parking on the grassland. In response to this complaint the local authority erected bollards to confine cars to a small, previously unfenced, car park at the southern end of the site. This angered locals who traditionally had been able to use an unfenced track leading from this car park to another at the more popular and sheltered northern end of the beach. The Council bollards had also illegally blocked a right of way. The bollards survived 48 hours before locals used heavy machinery to destroy them. The "obvious" solution of fencing both car parks and the track linking them is problematic because cattle must be allowed to move freely over the dunes (in the interests of both farmer and dune ecology). Fencing the track would not allow this unless cattle grids or gaps are used. Currently the issue remains unresolved.

Photo 43. Colour infrared view of Culdaff, Co. Donegal. Parts of the dunefield have been converted for use as a car park, access road and a leased playing field. The dark red of the playing field grasses contrasts with the lighter tone of the marram-dominated dunes.

"do the right thing". Public bodies habitually prefer to negotiate and compromise rather than use their full powers of formal enforcement, or have recourse to court action. This approach can be defended on the grounds that it is flexible and sensitive to local concerns, but it is more often true that long-term sustainability is sacrificed to achieve a relatively short-term solution. An unfortunate consequence of the prevailing ethos of compromise is the growth of a general perception that the statutory authorities are weak, lacking in conviction and indecisive. This in turn has contributed to a civic culture where blatant disregard for planning and environmental laws is commonplace.

Socio-economic pressures can have direct implications for specific coastal stretches. In order to increase employment opportunities the responsible authority will often allow and even encourage commercial, recreational and industrial development, even if environmental values and best practice in planning have to be compromised (see case study 22). This is exacerbated in remote areas where unemployment levels are high. At the local level one of the realities of coastal management is that major national and regional scale concerns are often secondary to local priorities. Owners of coastal lands, especially joint and public owners, are susceptible to public pressure to allow use for "community"

5. Devising a beach management plan - a guide for action

Why do it?

A management plan provides a means of realising the potential of a beach, whether as a resort or as a wilderness area, and of sustaining it for future generations. Without a formal management plan a beach may suffer from unregulated use and unsustainable processes. The harmful effects of this may become so serious that the damage is irreparable and the site loses its value as an amenity or as a natural system.

Who does it?

A management plan could be prepared by a number of bodies: a local community or development group; a special interest local group e.g. a golf or boat club; a developer as a condition for obtaining planning permission; a local authority; a statutory agency; a consultancy firm acting for a local authority or statutory agency; a conservation NGO; a university or other academic institution; a private operator. On balance, regardless of who commissions the study, the plan is most likely to be successful if it involves a partnership between different bodies such as community groups, local authorities and coastal scientists. This involvement should provide the broadest range of support, expertise and resources for the plan.

How to fund it?

Funding possibilities include the following: funds locally generated by a community group from donations and fund-raising activities; a national agency, e.g. a state tourist board; a local authority; developers; an NGO; any of the above in partnership with a European Community programme; grants from dedicated bodies e.g. International Fund for Ireland; charges from beach parking; voluntary levy on beach related businesses.

Steps in devising a beach management plan

The following steps are designed to act as guidelines for the process of strategic, proactive beach management. The main purpose is to make it more systematic. Reactive beach management is a quite different process and requires a different approach. Some of the earlier stages outlined below would not be as important when dealing with management issues in a reactive way.

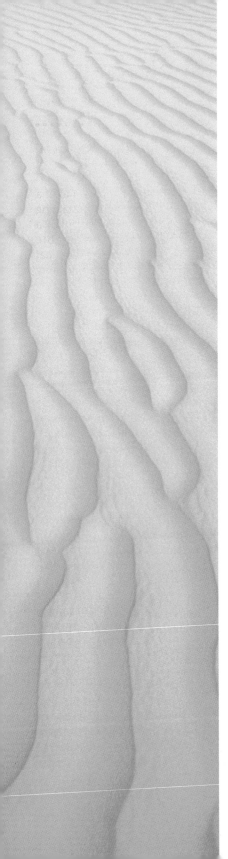

The steps outlined below are an example and would not necessarily need to be strictly adhered to in all cases. Other steps have been suggested (see, for example, Eurosite 1999). Depending on the circumstances, some steps will be more important than others and will therefore require more attention. However, there are certain principles, which are fundamental to the development of successful management plans, that should be observed. Plan development should, as far as possible, be systematic, inclusive, and based on objective analyses of the physical and human processes involved. An effective management plan should be based on facts, whether these concern the physical nature of the site or aspects of its human use. Most rural beaches have never been studied at all, while many others have often received only cursory attention in a piece of work undertaken many years earlier, e.g. an undergraduate dissertation. For this reason the formulation of a management plan may often require preliminary studies directed at elucidating the physical and human processes operating on the site.

The steps outlined below are:

1. Scoping
2. Launch
3. Preliminary studies
4. Identify aims
5. Decide on objectives
6. Identify ways of achieving objectives
7. Discussion
8. Select approach
9. Devise and circulate draft action plans
10. Implement
11. Review

1. SCOPING - at an early stage the scope of the plan needs to be defined. Decisions need to be made regarding what the plan's limits will be in terms of spatial extent, management remit, time scale, responsibility, involvement, liability and the degree of detail required. These decisions will depend on time available, cost-effectiveness considerations, skills possessed by the personnel involved, and the amount of previous work on the site. There is a continuum in the complexity of management plans ranging from fast descriptive approaches to those that take a lot more time and involve detailed quantitative survey and assessment requiring specialist personnel and equipment. The nature of any preliminary studies that are to be carried out should be decided at an early stage. Attempts should also be made to identify other beach management initiatives and those individuals and organisations with responsibility for any aspect of the site.

2. LAUNCH - the intention to devise a beach management plan should be made public. Open meetings are useful to raise the profile of the plan, make contacts and to gain some feedback regarding what people consider to be the issues at the site. Informal follow-up meetings with individuals may arise from the launch. These provide an opportunity to discuss specific issues with knowledgeable people, obtain information resources and get a feel for the character of the site.

3. PRELIMINARY STUDIES - these should be carried out (if required and practical), to gain some understanding of the physical and human processes at work and to identify potential management issues. In some cases it may be sufficient to use a qualitative "expert-eye" approach. A study may involve a search for all available previous literature on the site. This will include scientific studies such as academic theses and reports by statutory bodies and/or their consultants, and also more general work such as descriptions in travel books and historical accounts. All relevant studies done by statutory agencies and consultants such as Environmental Impact Assessments (EIAs) for sewerage and water schemes, port extensions, dredging and so on will be acquired and assessed. Other sources may include work done by local community groups or individuals. Part of this phase will be the collation of maps, charts, aerial and oblique photos from as many dates as possible. Assistance will be needed from libraries, local authorities and statutory bodies to unearth these materials.

Photo 44. Use of a Global Positioning System (GPS) to carry out a beach survey at Lisfannon, Co. Donegal.

A physical/geomorphological study may be carried out in order to describe the site and then determine its natural variability (see photo 44). Repeated surveys of selected cross-shore beach profiles will elucidate the contemporary variability of beach volume. Comparison of the present shoreline position with earlier positions taken from maps and aerial photographs will help determine whether the site is stable, eroding or accreting. If eroding it is important to know whether erosion is cyclic or progressive. If cyclic it is important to get some idea of the spatial envelope of change; if progressive it is important to know the rate of shoreline retreat. Rates of change and the envelope of change together form vital physical information required by subsequent site management. Past and contemporary sources, including anecdotal information, can be used to assess past and present human impact on these physical processes. The geomorphological study may include wave simulation modelling and this will require bathymetric, tidal, wave and wind data from relevant national authorities and private bodies (the ECOPRO manual (Government of Ireland, 1996) gives further guidance on carrying out surveys).

Photo 45. Ecological survey at Lisfannon, Co. Donegal.

An ecological study may be required to assess the habitat quality of the site in terms of the plant and animals species present. This may include studies of fauna, e.g. rabbit populations, birds and insects. It will cover the impacts of certain human uses including farming practices past and present e.g. marram harvesting, seaweed collection, deliberate firing, and former agricultural practices including past stocking rates. The effects of current management practices will be covered including recreational use, the effects of recreational and/or environmental designations, environmental conservation schemes, subsidies and current stocking rates. Study methods can range from quick descriptive overviews to detailed quantitative quadrat work (see photo 45) and habitat mapping according to accepted standard classifications (see, for example, Kent and Coker 1994). Modern GIS techniques can portray this information graphically (see figure 6).

An assessment of the human dimension at a site may also be necessary. This can involve studying visitor demographics, people's attitudes to and perceptions and knowledge of the site, and also studying the ways in which people use and interact with the site. For example, it may be useful to find out what people like or dislike about a beach, what they see as the potential problems, why they visit it at certain times etc. Central to this will be a survey of contemporary human use; however an historical perspective can be gained if earlier studies are available for comparison. The study can make use of data from tourist authorities, local development groups, published and unpublished academic materials; indeed previous work of any kind. Where the existing information is inadequate, a range of techniques can be employed to investigate the social context. Among these are questionnaires, interviews and observation. The choice of technique will depend on the aim of the research and the researchers' experience and preferences. There are many books that explain in detail the different approaches and techniques that can be used in social research (see for example: Oppenheim 1992; Cohen and Manion 1994).

4. IDENTIFY AIM(S) - decide on the overall vision for the site and state the underlying assumptions, e.g. "the overall aim is to develop a well-managed resort type beach because there is a need for a resort beach in the area and the system has already been developed in an unplanned and unsatisfactory way and has little recoverable wilderness character". Identifying and consulting stakeholders is required when deciding on the vision for the site. Rientjes (2000) gives some advice on identifying and communicating with stakeholders. This consultation should also serve to raise the profile of the plan and encourage people to become involved.

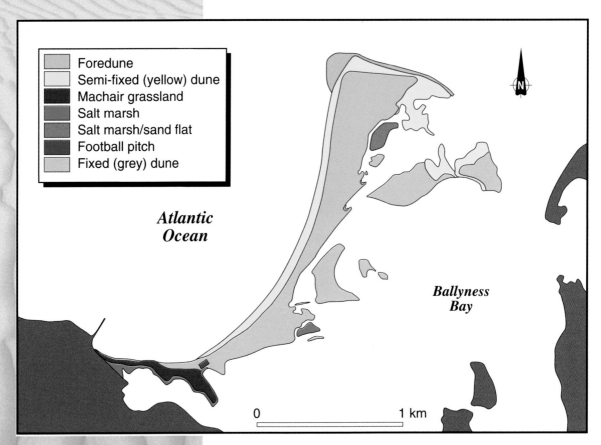

Legend:
- Foredune
- Semi-fixed (yellow) dune
- Machair grassland
- Salt marsh
- Salt marsh/sand flat
- Football pitch
- Fixed (grey) dune

Atlantic Ocean

Ballyness Bay

N

0   1 km

Figure 6. Habitat maps based on ecological surveys are useful tools in beach and dune management. This one was produced for the Dooey Peninsula at Magheraroarty, Co. Donegal.

5. DECIDE ON OBJECTIVES - formulate a range of specific objectives that provide a way of satisfying the overall aim and dealing with any issues highlighted in the preliminary studies, e.g. "improve the car parking facilities", or "reduce the amount of litter on the site". Indicate how the objectives relate to the overall aim for the site.

6. IDENTIFY MEANS - identify the different means of achieving each objective. For example, litter could be reduced in a number of ways such as providing more litter bins, increasing the frequency of collections, or by employing a litter warden. Chapter 4 of this guide provides some background information on ways of addressing various issues that occur in beach management.

7. DISCUSSION - a report describing the site and the processes at work, and outlining the aim and objectives of the plan should be produced and made available to all those interested. The report should outline the different ways of achieving the objectives. This should be done as objectively as possible with the advantages and disadvantages of each, probable costs, and lead agency identified. The discussion document should avoid making recommendations, except on non-controversial topics. The document should be in a

Photo 46. Public meeting at Rossnowlagh, Co. Donegal to discuss the development of a beach management plan for the site.

format and language suitable for a general audience, e.g. technical academic terms should be avoided as much as possible. Nevertheless accuracy should not be compromised. On issues like place names it is very important not to offend local sensibilities by failing to respect local custom and practice. Ground lost at this stage may be difficult to make up later. Where there is disagreement local practice, rather than secondary sources, should be followed. Stakeholders should be encouraged to provide feedback on the report, and express their preferred course of action. Feedback could be provided at public meetings or through other channels such as written responses. It should be borne in mind that problems can arise when meetings are not attended by major stakeholders such as landowners. There is also the risk that meetings (see photo 46) can be dominated by a few people. There is a fundamental problem involved in balancing the interests of those who live (and work) near the site all year round with those of visitors who come only a few times per year. Assessing the wishes of stakeholders can be difficult and sensitive, so it is therefore important to design the assessment carefully in order to avoid excluding any group or misrepresenting the public mood. At more complex sites, the use of formal, consensus building techniques may be necessary.

8. SELECT APPROACH - the appropriate combination of ways for achieving the objectives should be selected based on the reports and the feedback on them. This will involve assessing the acceptability, effectiveness (pilot studies, testing and expert advice may be required to assess the technical effectiveness of the options), and feasibility of the approaches. Feasibility depends on the available resources (which may need to be audited), and the possible constraints, whether financial, legal, temporal, physical, knowledge-based or other.

9. DEVISE AND CIRCULATE DRAFT ACTION PLANS - plans for implementation should be devised. The plans will be more focussed documents than the discussion documents as they will deal only with chosen options. Drafts should be examined for legal implications. The views of statutory bodies should be sought at the draft stage, e.g. authorities responsible for SACs or responsible for Blue Flag awards. The plans should indicate specific actions, the person(s) or bodies responsible for their execution, time scales for implementation and evaluation procedures. These should be disseminated, amended if necessary, then implemented.

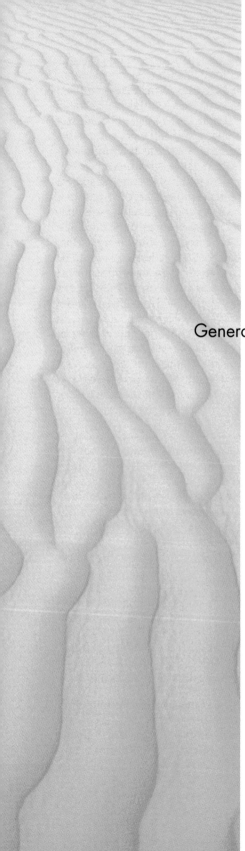

10. IMPLEMENTATION - the specific actions should be carried out according to the plans. If the resources are not available to implement all the actions then some prioritisation will be required. The implementation should be monitored and evaluated at regular intervals. If an action is not meeting its objectives then efforts should be made to establish the reasons behind this and take remedial action.

11. PLAN REVIEW - the whole plan should be reviewed periodically to establish whether or not it is achieving its objectives and overall aim(s). This review should take changing circumstances into account and amend the plan in light of these. For instance an increase in visitor numbers or a change in sediment transport patterns may necessitate amendments to the objectives or actions. It may be necessary to return to step 5 in light of the review and work through the steps again.

General points

Throughout the process sites need to be monitored for one-off events and changing trends. It is also important to keep the profile of the project high and make efforts to identify and involve stakeholders. A variety of techniques can be used to engage people with the project, such as brochures, illustrated reports, public meetings, open days, field trips, the internet, and local and national media. Other groups engaged in similar projects should be consulted and kept informed of progress, as should those with responsibility for aspects of the site. They should be invited to meetings and sent project documents. It is worth persevering with this, even if there is no obvious response, as it helps to maintain goodwill and interest and may facilitate collaboration at a later stage.

An active link is required with the local authority responsible for beach management, as they can be an invaluable source of information, contacts and support. This is especially true when the local authority has commissioned the management plan or is a partner in the project. The contact person should not be at too high a level in the local authority hierarchy as such a person will be too busy and often inaccessible. The best approach may be to have two contacts, one at a relatively low level for accessing documents and other general day-to-day work, and a higher level contact who can provide occasional executive authority when it is needed.

Concluding remarks

This Good Practice Guide arose primarily from lessons learned during a three-year demonstration project in coastal management carried out on seven rural beaches in County Donegal in northwest Ireland. It emphasizes the need to understand and work in harmony with natural and cultural processes operating at the coast. Our experience has taught us that lengthy research projects are not always needed to provide the understanding necessary to address every management issue. A great wealth of largely untapped knowledge already exists within coastal communities. Ideally, this should be coupled with objective and up-to-date baseline information in the form of maps, inventories and monitoring data. Unfortunately, in Ireland and elsewhere, such information is rarely available at a scale appropriate for site level management. Given this deficiency, case studies and experience in similar situations provide the best guide for decision-makers. This volume provides detailed practical examples that demonstrate how issues such as access, habitat management, shoreline erosion and zoning of activities may be resolved. While we hope we have encountered and discussed many of the problems facing managers on other rural coasts, each area presents a different set of pressures and constraints, and as a result, requires a unique set of strategies for sustainable management.

One of the key findings of our study in Donegal was that the current institutional framework and philosophy for managing coastal resources was not working adequately. At present, the local authority and national government agencies are expected to manage and protect coastal resources as part of their statutory responsibilities. However, on rural coasts, human and financial resources devoted to coastal management are rarely sufficient for the length of coastline, and the level of development and visitor pressure that the coast is experiencing. In Donegal, where institutional resources are severely lacking, managers are forced to adopt an *ad hoc*, reactive model, with positive measures confined to a small number of sites such as Natura 2000 and Blue Flag beaches. Large sections of coast are neglected, and as a result have become degraded or subject to inappropriate or illegal development. This situation is obviously detrimental to both the long-term maintenance of natural processes, and the continued attractiveness of the county as a holiday and recreational area.

It is clear from our experiences in Donegal that the intensive, institutionally-driven management approach of English "resort" towns or National Trust properties is neither feasible nor desirable on rural beaches. The resident population is too small and dispersed, and the holiday season too short and volatile, to justify the large increases in local authority spending that would bring coastal management up to the level required on fully-developed coasts or on nature reserves. The present low numbers of

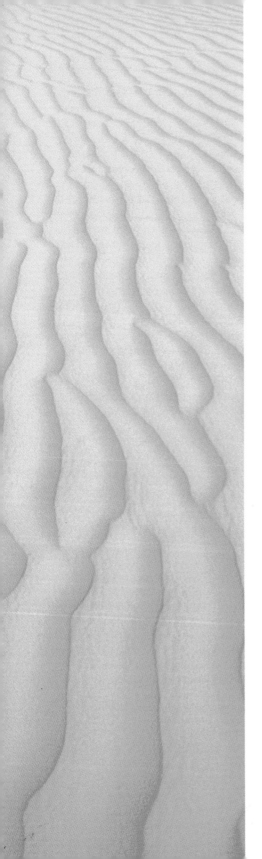

environmental managers in the county is likely to remain - there are currently no trained coastal managers with the local authority. In addition, only five wildlife rangers patrol thousands of hectares of habitat, including hundreds of kilometres of coast. In order to achieve more sustainable coastal management, the energy, enthusiasm and goodwill of the resident and visitor communities must be harnessed to complement government and local authority efforts. We hope that this volume provides some inspiration and guidance for the development of co-management schemes, whereby partnerships are forged between statutory management agencies and the people living in and using coastal areas. We would welcome any feedback on its contents.

References

Atkinson, D. and Houston, J. (eds.) (1993), The Sand Dunes of the Sefton Coast. Proceedings of the Sefton Coast Research Seminar, Liverpool, 31st May 1991, National Museums & Galleries on Merseyside/Sefton Metropolitan Borough Council.

Binggeli, P., Eakin, M., Macfadyen, A., Power, J. and McConnell, J. (1992), Impact of the alien sea buckthorn (*Hippophae rhamnoides* L.) on sand dune ecosystems in Ireland. In: Carter, R.W.G., Curtis, T.G.F. and Sheehy-Skeffington, M.J. (eds.) Coastal Dunes: Geomorphology, Ecology and Management for Conservation. Balkema, Rotterdam. 325-337.

Brady Shipman Martin (1997), Coastal Zone Management: A Draft Policy for Ireland. Government of Ireland, Dublin.

Brooks, A. (1979 revd. 1986), Sand Dunes: A Practical Handbook. British Trust for Conservation Volunteers, Wallingford.

Cambers, Gillian (1998), Coping With Beach Erosion: with Case Studies from the Caribbean. UNESCO, Paris

Carter, R.W.G. (1988), Coastal Environments: An Introduction to the Physical, Ecological and Cultural Systems of Coastlines. Academic Press, London.

Carter, R.W.G., Eastwood, D.A. and Bradshaw, Philip (1992), Small scale sediment removal from beaches in Northern Ireland: environmental impact, community perception and conservation management. Aquatic Conservation: Marine and Freshwater Ecosystems, 2, (1), 95-113.

CERC (1984), Shore Protection Manual. US Army Corps of Engineers, US Government Printing Office, Washington, DC.

CHL (2000), Coastal Engineering Manual. US Army Corps of Engineers, US Government Printing Office, Washington, DC.

Cohen, L. and Manion, L. (1994), Research Methods in Education (4th edition). Routledge, London.

Crosbie, John (1995), Coastal Zone Legislation in Ireland and Changes Needed. In: Carroll, M. and Dubsky, K. (eds.) Coastal Zone Management: From Needs to Action, Proc. Conference, Dublin, Ireland, 3-6 Sep. 1994. Coastwatch Europe Network, Trinity College Dublin, 227-232.

Department of the Environment, Transport and the Regions (UK) (1998), Review of Byelaw Powers for the Coast: Report of the Inter-Departmental Working Party. DETR, London.

Donegal County Council (2000), County Donegal Development Plan (3 vols.). DCC, Lifford, Co. Donegal.

Edwards, S.D., Jones, P.S. and Nowell, D.E. (1997), Participation in Coastal Zone Management Initiatives: A Review and Analysis of Examples from the UK. Ocean and Coastal Management, 36, (1-3), 143-65.

European Commission (1999 a), Towards a European Integrated Coastal Zone Management (ICZM) Strategy: General Principles and Policy Options: Office for Official Publications of the European Communities, Luxembourg.

European Commission (1999 b), Lessons from the European Commission's Demonstration Programme on Integrated Coastal Zone Management (ICZM). Office for Official Publications of the European Communities, Luxembourg.

Eurosite (1999), Eurosite Management Planning Toolkit. Eurosite Secretariat, Wimereux, France.

Gibson, John (1999), Legal and Regulatory Bodies: Appropriateness to Integrated Coastal Zone Management. Final Report., Contract B5-9500/97/000597/MAR//D2, European Commission-DG XI.D.2, (Available at http://europa.eu.int/comm/environment/iczm/themanal.htm)

Government of Ireland (1996), ECOPRO: Environmentally Friendly Coastal Protection.The Stationery Office, Dublin.

Hickie, David (1996), Evaluation of Environmental Designations in Ireland. The Heritage Council, Dublin.

Kay, R. and Alder, J. (1999), Coastal Planning and Management. E and FN Spon, London.

Kelley, J. T., Kelley, A.R. and Pilkey, O.H. (1989), Living with the Coast of Maine. Duke University Press, Durham/London.

Kent, M. and Coker, P. (1994), Vegetation Description and Analysis: A Practical Approach. John Wiley & Sons, Chichester.

Lencek, L. and Bosker, G. (1999), The Beach: The History of Paradise on Earth. Pimlico, London.

MacLeod, M., Cooper, A., Mc Kenna, J., Power, J. and O'Hagan, A. M. (2000), The Potential of a Legislative Approach to Managing Beach Use: The Case of Beach Bye-Laws in the Republic of Ireland. Coastal Management, 28, 363-382.

Nordstrom, K.F. (2000), Beaches and Dunes of Developed Coasts. Cambridge University Press, Cambridge.

Oates, M., Harvey, H.J. and Glendell, M. (eds.) (1998), Grazing Sea Cliffs and Dunes for Nature Conservation. The National Trust Estates Department, Cirencester.

Oppenheim, A. N. (1992), Questionnaire Design, Interviewing and Attitude Measurement (2nd edition). Pinter Publishers, London.

Pethick, John (1984), An Introduction to Coastal Geomorphology. Edward Arnold, London.

Power, J, Mc Kenna, J., MacLeod, M.J., Cooper, J.A.G. and Convie, G. (2000), Developing Integrated Participatory Management Strategies for Atlantic Dune Systems in County Donegal, Northwest Ireland. Ambio, 29, (3), 143-49.

Quinn, A.C.M. (1977), Sand Dunes: Formation, Erosion and Management. An Foras Forbartha, Dublin.

Rientjes, S. (ed.) (2000), Communicating Nature Conservation. European Centre for Nature Conservation, Tilburg.

Royal Society for the Protection of Birds (1998), Red Card for Blue Flags? Sixth Sense (the RSPB magazine). October 1998.

Stranks, J. (1997), A Manager's Guide to Health and Safety at Work. Kogan Page, London.

Sturgess, P.W. (1993), Clear-Felling Dune Plantations: Studies in Vegetation Recovery on the Sefton Coast. In: Atkinson, D. and Houston, J. (eds.). The Sand Dunes of the Sefton Coast. Proceedings of the Sefton Coast Research Seminar, Liverpool, 31st May 1991. National Museums & Galleries on Merseyside/Sefton Metropolitan Borough Council, 85-89.